DANCING WITH LAWYERS

How to Take Charge and Get Results

NICHOLAS CARROLL

 ROYCE BAKER PUBLISHING

Published by Royce Baker Publishing, Inc.
953 Mountain View Drive, Lafayette, California 94549

Printed in the United States of America

FIRST EDITION

Library of Congress Cataloging-in-Publication Data

Carroll, Nicholas, date.
  Dancing with lawyers: How to take charge and get results.
Nicholas Carroll. — 1st ed.
    p. cm.
  Includes bibliographical references.
  ISBN 1-879435-03-9
    1. Attorney and client — United States—Popular works.
2. Lawyers—United States—Popular works.   I. Title.
KF311.Z9C37 1991
340'.023—dc20   90-64419

To Jane Edmisten,
who carries her clients
the extra miles.

ACKNOWLEDGEMENTS

With thanks to:

Warren Benson
Alice Covington
Ruth Crawford
Martin Fraser
William Friedman
Robert Ghelerter
Monica Gillham
Patricia Haskell
Carole Klein
Chris Kralj
Susan Kralj
Nancy Skinner
Nancy Sutton

DISCLAIMER

The author is not an attorney, and neither publisher nor author is providing legal advice, or any guarantee that this generalized information will have the intended results in a specific situation. If the reader has a specific legal question he should consult an expert.

INTRODUCTION

People enter law school for a variety of reasons: The pursuit of justice—or power; to change the world—or feed off it; to get the respect they deserve—or lord it over secretaries; to make their parents happy; to (mistakenly) get a general education; to prolong school and delay work; to make big money; and on occasion, because law interests them. Many of them do not intend to practice law. Most do.

Though they start for different reasons, life beyond the entry exams is much the same from school to school. So is the entry-level work afterwards. The training involves a way of thought more than the study of facts. The hours are long, and ambition is high. They have limited time or inclination for outside interests; law becomes reality. They are taught to argue—endlessly. Their sense of humor erodes; original goals are forgotten. The strange and meaningless rules they obey gradually close the doors of imagination. It remains true that "The law sharpens a mind by narrowing it."

A product of legal education is likely to be the most troublesome temporary employee you will ever hire. This book is about managing these employees; about getting results out of them; and—when possible—controlling their appetite for money.

Some readers will ask, "Aren't there any honest lawyers?" Of course; even with a rigid definition of honesty, you'll find some honest lawyers. There are even a few lawyers who break all the stereotypes; I deal with one whom I suspect of being a genuine hippie. But this book is not about the evils of lawyers. It is about the strange attitudes of lawyers, about getting the job done, about money, about the struggle to get what you want, about taking charge; it is about dancing with lawyers.

- There is evidence to support and contradict almost every opinion in this book. My file cabinets are packed with both kinds. Yet debate is of little use to the reader who asks "how?"—and with that in mind, there are few footnotes.

- Likewise there are few anecdotes. Though I've included a few, anecdotes too often carry a fatal weakness: they describe things that happened to someone else. It's often hard to make the leap back to your own situation. Anyhow, if you intend to hire a lawyer, you don't need my anecdotes. You'll have your own soon enough. I hope that forewarned, you will look back in humor.

- *Job* means anything you hire a lawyer for. When feeling precise, I use *task* (a single, defined job, usually small), or *project* (many tasks that add up to a complicated job).

- I like the word "customer" better than "client."
    customer *n.*   1. a patron, shopper, or buyer
    client *n.*   1. a person under protection of another: VASSAL, DEPENDENT 2. in Rome, a plebeian under protection of a patrician

- I've used "he" to denote both men and women. My original draft attempted to avoid this convention; after endless re-writes failed to make the manuscript readable, I returned to the traditional style.

Nicholas Carroll
San Francisco
June 17th, 1991

HOW TO USE THIS BOOK

Read: The INTRODUCTION
            ADOPT AN ATTITUDE, p. 33
            PROJECT MANAGEMENT, p. 85
            A UNIVERSAL THEORY OF BILL CONTROL, p. 130
            THE CHART, p. 176

Those contain the basic ideas. If you're about to hire, read the FINDING AND HIRING section (p.91) as well.

Then browse. If you don't find what you want, try another chapter. The format of the book should make sense when you look at the table of contents. The chapters are short for two reasons:

1. So experienced customers can go directly to the subject that interests them.

2. So inexperienced customers don't have to try and digest the entire book as one chunk. The human mind doesn't work that way; it absorbs by bits and pieces and then creates its own understanding.

Even if you could absorb a book in one sitting, you can't have confidence in an idea until it *belongs* to you. For this reason the "business" attitude is repeated throughout the book. If you read the message enough times it will begin to seem like a normal and sensible way to deal with a lawyer. And it is normal; many, many customers take this attitude. You want to be one of them.

CONTENTS

WHO YOU NEED TO BE

HOW TO GET THE JOB DONE

Basics

DANCING
WITH
LAWYERS

ADVISOR TO THE UNIVERSE

Lawyers believe they are equipped to offer advice to anyone. This belief is founded on several notions: that they are more intelligent than the rest of us; that law is civilization's supreme system of order; and that "learning to think like a lawyer" has equipped them with the finest possible tools to analyze human affairs, both big and small.

The belief is ill-proven, because until they've given up thinking like lawyers, they don't do well in other fields (with the unfortunate exception of politics).

Aside from the peculiar belief that law describes reality, lawyers are simply not well-rounded people. They work long hours, and they spend their limited free time thinking about law. As a consequence, their expertise is in law, and only in law. Beyond that their knowledge consists of what the customers have told them in their office, but this is disorganized data; they rarely think it out.

For business advice, try friends in business; for personal advice, try your grandmother.

ARROGANCE AND EGOTISM

Arrogance grows in law school, where the future lawyers develop it as a defense against overbearing professors and unpleasant fellow-students. It flowers on the first job, when the junior associates find they're still being treated shabbily. Timid customers keep feeding it.

Arrogance includes the desire to make other people feel inferior; the arrogant always need victims. An employee like that probably isn't worth hiring.

Egotism is less common than arrogance, and sometimes less troublesome; in a competent human, egotism tends to be focused on the job, not the customers.

If your lawyer is a competent egotist, live with it. Just don't let it grow on you.

BALLFIELD, THE WRONG ONE

ballfield, *n.* 3. *slang* the general situation.

There is only one way to start a job: Find out what the customer wants. It means good listening, but it also means asking the right questions. Lawyers are famous for overrunning this base. They snap out the questions, scribble on a pad, and start telling you what you're going to do.

The result is that three minutes into describing your problem, you may not recognize the problem anymore. Is the lawyer running around the wrong ballfield?

Customers who know exactly what they want can minimize this distraction, by immediately revealing the purpose of the visit.

Beginners may want to let the lawyer run a bit, and take notes. Then as he rushes to the conclusion and begins to end the conversation, look at your original notes (the situation as you saw it) and return to the beginning of the conversation.

When you have both views of the situation in plain view, you can move on to a decision.

BREEDING LITIGATION

It happens. And it happens more often than it used to.

Many people assume that lawyers generate trouble just so they can charge for it. This ain't necessarily so. The thought process doesn't have to go that far. Bird dogs find birds; lawyers find problems. Beavers build endless dams; lawyers build endless contracts. Groundhogs dig holes; lawyers dig holes.

Lawyers can breed litigation whether they're thinking of money or not. Don't assume your lawyer is avoiding useless conflict just because he's competent or honest.

BUSINESS ABILITY, JUDGMENT, AND KNOWLEDGE

BUSINESS ABILITY

Not much. When lawyers are actually involved in some other type of business—and personally facing consequences—they make bad decisions. Blunders come in many forms: penny wise, pound foolish; tantrums; sensitivity with people who need firmness; arrogance with people who need diplomacy.

Basically, lawyers have little trade sense, and they don't use the little they have. (They are frequently good with financial calculations. This is a useful skill—lawyers have kept many overeager customers out of bad deals. But calculating and *finding opportunity* in the calculations are not at all the same thing.)

Lawyers like to debate about their business ability, pointing out that they make a lot of money. The answer: so would ditch-diggers, if they had a guild system boosting prices to $150 an hour—and billed the customers separately for shovels and shoes.

I'm disconcerted (but not surprised) that the debaters never seem to notice the lawyers who own most of the business ability—the ones who left law and now run restaurants, ice cream parlor chains, and publishing houses. These former lawyers have points in common: they don't see themselves as lawyers anymore, and they seem to be generating more fun and money than they could in law.

BUSINESS JUDGMENT

Yes and no. Since lawyers see a great deal of folly, they often have a good sense of what sort of transactions lead to trouble. Take note of any *concrete* warnings that come out of their experience with sour deals. (This isn't just business. House sales, divorces, and estates can be very sour deals indeed.)

Unfortunately, lawyers don't take an active interest in their customers; they never really learn about people. Between that and their lack of hands-on business experience, you can't really expect them to give good advice on what you should do.

As business judgment goes, there are three levels. You'll have to decide which level the lawyer is operating at. I'd reckon that:

- One in 100 can create a business solution.

- One in 50 can ask: "So have you got all the business questions worked out?" In other words, "You're the business expert, I'm the legal expert. Tell me when it's time to do my job " (A good lawyer will speak up when you're about to cut your own throat—but also knows when to wait.)

- The rest don't have business judgment, but usually think they do.

It would be nice if you could just lay it all out on a lawyer's table, and brain-storm the possibilities; an employee who looks at the big picture is generally an asset, whether it's the vice-president or a mail-room clerk. This approach rarely works with lawyers. They usually can't get their minds out of the legal rut long enough to understand the big picture—and they take your open approach as a request for guidance.

Furthermore, trying to educate them is a mighty expensive experiment, since they charge for time spent learning. Frequently you end up extracting the knowledge you need item by item, and assembling the big picture in your own mind.

BUSINESS KNOWLEDGE

Lots. Lawyers are constantly seeing deals go down. True, they're far from mind-readers, but they see the transactions: how much their customers are paying for office space, whether free parking usually comes with the deal, and what the typical lease period is. Unfortunately they don't realize how valuable the knowledge is, preferring to think about what might happen legally, instead of what is actually happening in the real world.

The ones who know that they're legal experts are usually better at giving you business facts than the ones who think they're universal experts. The legal expert may neglect to offer the facts unless you ask him, but the universal expert often squirrels them away until he gets the chance to impress.

CUSTOMERS—FROM THE LAWYER'S VIEW

According to lawyers, customers:

- Unload their stress on the lawyer, and then ignore the problem.

- Don't answer the lawyer's letters.

- Set unreasonable deadlines which cause the lawyer to work grueling overtime.

- Regularly mistake their lawyer for a psychiatrist, or even a chauffeur. (No lawyers have given me the details, for which I'm grateful.)

- Lose respect for the lawyer when the bill is too low—a $500 bill means this is a $500 lawyer; if the customer later has a $5,000 job, they'll figure it's too big for him, and go find a $5,000 lawyer.

- Lose respect for lawyers who make things too simple.

Then there are the things lawyers believe all customers want:

- Reassurance and guidance.

- A lawyer who seems busy (hence in demand).

- A lawyer who devotes energy to the job.

- Lots of copies in the mail.

- Letters and bills on engraved stationery.

- An answering service instead of an answering machine, even though the customer may know perfectly well that the lawyer is a sole practitioner with no secretary.

Unfortunately, there's truth to both the complaints and the beliefs. If you want nothing but results, at a good price, you're part of the minority. The majority is misusing lawyers, as well as letting the lawyers misuse them. A minority won't change the paternalistic world-view of the legal establishment—but there are lawyers willing to make an exception to that world-view, once a businesslike customer gets their attention. If the lawyer notices that you meet the criteria in WHAT LAWYERS RESPECT (p.32), you'll get a certain amount of attention anyway.

EFFICIENCY, LACK OF

Efficiency is to some extent a process of cooperation, even among the most competitive people. Law school teaches the adversary system (explained in ADVERSARY SYSTEM, p.49).

Despite that, lawyers might have learned efficiency in law school. They didn't. Law schools don't teach project management, bookkeeping, computer skills . . . in fact, they don't teach a single course related to productivity, and very few aimed at results for the customer. So the lawyers get their business know-how out of personnel manuals, which instruct them in the art of managing legal secretaries.

End result: inefficiency.

Lawyers do work long and hard, but:

• Long hours aren't the same as efficiency.

• Hard work isn't the same as efficiency.

• And profit for the law firm definitely isn't the same as efficiency.

FEARS OF LAWYERS

Lawyers fear:

- Loss of the client. The smallest of their fears. (Lawyers tell me it's the biggest fear; I assure you it's not.)

- Loss of control (over the situation, you, their secretary, and anything else that comes to mind). Probably more than you do.

- Damage to their ego (including loss of face, and damage to their professional reputation). Probably much more than you do.

- Lawsuits. The public doesn't win that often, but even lawyers find lawsuits a burden.

- Disbarment. A very unlikely event, but the fear tends to lurk in the backs of their minds. A license is critical to their self-image. Without it they are no better than their customers.

Don't be misled by newspaper images of the high priests of law, the silver-haired Ivy League lawyers with political connections and hand-made suits. Where these types may—or may not—be bulletproof, a state regulatory agency could theoretically go after a garden-variety lawyer—possibly beyond disbarment, to criminal prosecution. Even the state bar associations have been known to throw their members to the wolves.

Disbarment lies close to death. Without engineering credentials, you can still engineer; without a law license, the closest you can come is working as an economy lawyer in a back room of some giant corporation.

There are very few lawyers in this country who haven't given serious thought to disbarment. Even lawyers on the way to another career don't want to be bounced.

HOW LAWYERS SEE YOU

Mostly, they don't. Once a lawyer adds up your profile, based on the points in WHAT LAWYERS RESPECT (p.32), the calculation is fairly well complete. If you're headed for court, he'll assess your potential as a witness. And if it looks like you're going to cry or become violent, he'll keep an eye on you.

This shouldn't be a complete surprise. After all, to a shoe salesman, you're a pair of feet and a wallet. It may be reasonable to expect more from a white-collar professional—but in the case of lawyers, don't.

This isn't all bad. How much do you want an employee to know about you?

HYSTERIA, CLIMATE OF

Creating hysteria gives lawyers a sense of importance—makes them feel like the eye of the hurricane, the hub of the wheel. It may not be done consciously, but if they make you agitated, they will indeed become the center of things.

You may not be able to keep a lawyer from his own hysteria, but at least don't let him agitate you, especially at the beginning (when you're deciding what needs doing). Walk the conversation back to your original purpose. It might cost more, but if you don't get the original questions answered, you've probably paid for nothing. If you want the lawyer to actually carry out a job, it's even more important to get him back on track.

Lawyers claim that customers are hysterical. That happens too. A common scenario: the lawyer starts out composed and becomes hysterical as the job approaches deadlines; the customer is hysterical on first contact and calms down with the notion that something is being done.

(Hysteria has another function: it drives lawyers to greater effort. This may even reduce a customer's bill; a twenty-hour job can get done in ten. I'm not comfortable with this method of bill reduction.)

See FAST STARTS *(p.66)*.

LAWYERS AS CUSTOMERS OR BUSINESS PARTNERS

Does this belong in a book on dancing with lawyers? Yes. Quite a few customers have hired a lawyer and ended up with that lawyer as one of their customers or partners.

LAWYERS AS CUSTOMERS

Lawyers can definitely be good customers. They're usually too busy to pester you, they charge their own customers a lot (which ought to mean they have money), and sometimes they're delighted to be talking to someone who's neither a lawyer nor a client.

They have some difficulties, however—which can be managed when you know what to expect.

They Assume They're Smarter Than You

This leads to a general attitude of dissatisfaction, as though your product is never *quite* right—but it isn't a problem as long as they don't have time to pester you. Ignore it.

They Get Testy, Sometimes Rude

Ignore it. If you have employees, tell them to ignore bad manners and refer the lawyer back to you.

They Look for Disagreements

It's their nature. It doesn't necessarily mean they intend to cheat you, but it can lead to dissatisfaction or renegotiation.

Stop it before it happens. Treat difficult lawyers as you would any difficult customer: take them through the job step by step, spell it out, make them repeat what you said, root out any misunderstandings. Make conversation notes or send letters of understanding if you're still concerned. If necessary sell them your very best product, so they won't have any quality points to complain about later.

Those first three problems apply whether a lawyer is buying something for his personal use or for his business.

The next problem tends to affect you only if you're providing something for a lawyer's business. But be careful with a big personal job, especially when working on his house.

Poor Cash Flow

Lawyers often have poor cash flow, either from mismanaging their money or from taking too many cases on contingency. When businesses run short of cash, they give priority to those who can put them out of business. Where do you fit in?

Third-Party Payment (strictly a business-to-business problem)

Lawyers see themselves as separate from the hustle and bustle of vulgar business. A lawyer will ask another business to provide a service—such as an estate appraisal—and when that business sends the bill, the lawyer tells them that they'll be paid directly by the client; or when the client pays the legal bill; or when the court authorizes the expense; or when the client succeeds in collecting a judgment.

When you persist they get snotty. Then they start ducking your phone calls.

These last two difficulties have given lawyers a reputation as deadbeats. A surprising number of them write rubber checks. (If you doubt this, ask a few bank tellers.) Make sure you get paid; collecting a deposit or payment in advance might be appropriate.

LAWYERS AS PARTNERS

Lawyers are good silent partners, at least initially. They're busy with their own work, and they respect your status as an expert.

Then they get a taste of the action. Hands on. For the first time they're not working as a consultant.

At about the same time, they realize they can understand the words you're using. That wouldn't be a problem, but for one thing—since the legal business is largely jargon, they assume jargon is also a main pillar of your business. To them this means they now understand your business.

At this point your credibility shrinks; you're no longer an expert. And the lawyer reckons he can handle the business as well as you can. (Better, actually, because he's a lawyer.)

You should think long and hard before going partners with anyone. Think a bit more if the prospective partner is a lawyer.

Ask yourself: Is there any danger he'll find enough time to help me run the business?

LAWYER-TO-LAWYER

There are three types of lawyer-to-lawyer interactions which have a life all of their own (they're not necessarily related to getting the job done):

- Fighting, whether in court or over contracts. Can lead to expense without results.

- Socializing, whether by telephone or letter or memo or conference. Can lead to expense without results.

- Less obvious is the routine squabbling: pulling rank, intimidation, trampling junior associates with partner power, needling each other in letters, deliberately leaving key phrases out of letters of agreement, and making unreasonable contract demands—buried in the second page.

It's mildly entertaining to hand someone else's lawyer a letter or contract (from your own lawyer) which contains a hidden insult, such as a flagrant loophole in your favor. The receiving lawyer will bounce around in his chair. He knows he's been insulted—and doesn't want a customer to know it. Which sets him to grumbling about ". . . not proper . . . isn't the right form . . . doesn't your lawyer know that . . ."

Mild entertainment ought to be the limit. It's OK to let the troops have fun. Some squabbling can be ignored, especially when your lawyer has more prestige (if your lawyer has less prestige, you'll have to break it up much sooner). In any case don't let them go so far it interferes with the job; fun has to stop before the feuding stage, because it can lead to—expense without results.

Martin Fraser, a friend who practices transaction law in London, has told me in complete sincerity, "When our law firm hires American lawyers, we have to be careful not to let them carry on frolics of their own."

LIES BY CUSTOMERS

In the course of practicing law, lawyers expect their customers to lie.
That's the way you should see it. Naturally some lawyers hear more lies
than others. (A lawyer who does nothing but write wills and contracts
may not hear any at all; the customers have little reason to lie until the
disagreements surface.)

But despite their training in advocacy, most lawyers want to believe
their customers. So they see the whole thing quite differently . . .

Case Study

Visualize a 24-year-old lawyer interviewing a hardened criminal. The
criminal tells his story. The young lawyer writes on a legal pad. The
criminal finishes; the lawyer stops writing. The lawyer now looks over
his pad, stares through the pad, imagining the trial. *This is not a winna-
ble case*, he realizes . . . *I need more information* . . . and begins ques-
tioning the criminal on areas of inconsistency. The criminal answers.
The lawyer, naturally being more intelligent and articulate, asks
pointed questions that clarify the facts ("You mean . . ."). Remember,
the prosecutor will be doing the same thing . . . Another page of notes,
and the defense has taken shape.

This is a customer and lawyer collaborating—creating a story designed
to bore the judge, stump the prosecutor, and satisfy the jury.

What the lawyer saw was the exercise of his legal skills: determining
the facts and weaving them into a coherent, integrated defense. The
prosecution will prosecute, the defense will defend, and in this best of
all legal systems, the truth will come out in court.

The criminal and the lawyer are in basic agreement: A tight story
equals a true story.

Visualize a 34-year-old lawyer interviewing a hardened criminal. The lawyer sets the tone of the interview, because clients don't always know what's important to a case. He asks the questions, and writes on a legal pad, as another part of his mind sees the courtroom. When the client rambles or provides irrelevant information, he cuts him off. He clarifies points when necessary, and asks the client to repeat them so there is no misunderstanding (". . . let me understand this . . ." he says . . .). At the end of the interview he sums up the case, gives the client a hard stare, and asks if there is anything else he needs to know, or "Is there anything else you need to tell me?"

This is an experienced criminal lawyer mapping out a customer's defense. He assembled the defense; at the same time he let the client know when to keep his mouth shut, coached him on the right answers, tested him to see if he could remember his lines in court, and asked if there were any nasty surprises that could blow them both out of the water. These latter techniques are part of what is known as "witness preparation."

With ten years of experience, and the right case, this could be a story that will leave the judge admiring, the prosecutor humiliated, and the jury sobbing.

What the lawyer saw was a case. As to whether it is right, that was established a long time ago, in law school: A tight story equals a true story.

(Criminal law is the most extreme example, but the pattern is the same for other types of lawyers.)

Telling a Lawyer the Whole Truth

Spitting out the whole truth may limit a lawyer's options. According to their professional ethics, lawyers are supposed to discourage clients from lying. The rules get more specific where courtroom perjury is concerned.

The vast majority of lawyers fall into one of two groups: those who would prefer to believe their customers, and those who don't care. The two groups have a common agenda, though: *they don't actually want to hear the confession*. A lawyer will be awfully reluctant to put a liar on the stand—even a superb liar. It's a fairly bold lawyer who'll say "Forget that happened," or "Shut up and say what I tell you to."

If the case isn't likely to reach the courtroom, a lawyer has more flexibility—but he still has to consider what might happen ten years from now. Almost anything could theoretically come back to haunt him.

Of course, everyone is "entitled to a spirited defense." And in fact, the legal defense may be a better bet than a factual defense.

There is a third group of lawyers—cynics take note—who actually want their customers to tell the truth at all times; for them *the legal system = justice = the customer's best interests*. However, most lawyers see themselves as "advocate" first, and "officer of the court" a distant second.

Pointless Lies

If the job is unlikely to end in court, a lawyer would just as soon not listen to a load of rubbish.

Deceiving a Lawyer

Some customers conclude that they have to give their lawyer the big lie—that the gap between the truth and the law is so wide that no lawyer could build a good case. Or—in a business deal—they may be using the lawyer to manipulate the competition. Other customers are simply naive, especially in civil cases, where the inexperienced sometimes believe the blue ribbon goes to whoever tells a better whopper. It's as though there were no witnesses, no contracts, no written records, no signatures, and no reality.

For whatever reason, these customers don't give the lawyer any discreet clues, like "It's a good thing I have a solid alibi. If I didn't, I'll bet that would really hurt the case, wouldn't it?" (Actually, that's not too discreet.)

This modus operandi moves into what all lawyers consider a lie—something that can explode in their faces, and make them look stupid. Lawyers, far more than the average human, hate to look stupid.

Customers who string a lawyer along sometimes assume the worst that can happen is the lawyer will be angry. Wrong. If a lawyer finds out before the job is finished, he may slack off or try to dump the customer (at a critical moment). He may also call up the opposition lawyer (who might be the D.A.) and try to cut any lousy deal at all—which he will then try to sell to his customer as a good deal. (If he goes this far, revenge is probably coming into play.)

When the Opposition Is Lying

When the opposition is the police, a lawyer should be able to accept the idea that they are lying.

Customers in civil cases sometimes have occasion to wonder whether their lawyer's head is screwed on tight—when he tells them that the opposition couldn't be lying, because ". . . their lawyer is a fine attorney who wouldn't stand for that." And this is ten minutes after he has finished his own customer's coaching session.

That isn't necessarily a time for panic. A lawyer's instinct is still to ferret out inconsistencies and weaknesses. And if a tight story is a true story, a loose story is an untrue story. As long as he doesn't show any other signs of insanity, just keep a close eye on him.

When the Opposition Is Lying Monstrously

Big lies can be a serious challenge to a lawyer's skills. They have no relation to reality, so it can be hard to contradict them with mere facts. They are usually uncomplicated, which means they are usually consistent (tight).

If the biggest lie of the decade is coming your way, don't count on your lawyer to handle it. Step back and look at the big picture. Be prepared to go dig up the evidence yourself.

The Limits of Lying

Don't get too excited with the possibilities of lying. It's not the only element of a case. There is also interpretation of the law. And of course, there is the opposition; they may have unsinkable facts.

LIES BY LAWYERS
(TO THEIR OWN CUSTOMERS*)

Lawyers lie a lot more than farmers, but less than used car salesmen; in short, you've heard worse. As a customer you should concentrate on when and where the lies occur.

At the Beginning of a Job

Exaggerating expertise. Slightly more common than in other service businesses. "Sure, we do that," followed by mumbo-jumbo when you try to find out just how often they do that. This is a clear warning of missing know-how, because there definitely are lawyers who'll say "That's all I do," or "I don't do that."

Promising unrealistic results is closely linked to exaggerating expertise.

Both these habits are more common in family law, personal injury, worker's compensation, tenant law, drunk driving, and immigration. Not surprisingly, these are specialties that typically serve poor or inexperienced customers.

Making the job sound harder than it is. Happens to rich and poor alike—sometimes to impress the customer, sometimes in preparation for a big bill. Of course, a lawyer who exaggerates the difficulty too much will *have* to write a big bill—or the customer will get suspicious about the difficulty.

*Customers have been content to let their lawyers lie *for* them for most of the 2,000 years since lawyers first offered the service. This agreement between customers and lawyers has been so fundamental that it can hardly be called a problem. More like an area of high customer satisfaction.

During a Job

Mistakes aren't a major source of lies. Why would they be? The customers usually don't spot the mistakes. Either they're camouflaged by the normal jargon and mumbo-jumbo of the legal trade, or the lawyers correct them before the ship sinks.

Delays. This area requires heavy doses of deception, because background camouflage won't work. Customers are working off the same calendar as the lawyers. But since customers rarely demand a hard timetable and task list—in advance—the lawyer can usually revise history to suit his needs.

If the job is headed for court, and the customer has a schedule, revision becomes riskier; the customer may compare the court papers against the calendar, or even drive down to the courthouse and look up the actual filing dates.

At the End

Billing is where 70% or 80% of the lies are found. By general business standards this is an unusual concentration. It's also to be expected. Lawyers are charging too much. The more a business overcharges, the more it has to lie at billing time.

LITIGATORS

It's a fairly common notion that lawyers love showing off in the courtroom. There are three more things to know:

- The litigator (civil trial lawyer) is actually a subspecies. Many lawyers never go to court and don't want to.

- There's no common mold to a litigator. Though most are visibly arrogant, many are introverts (or also introverts).

- There's no certainty of how he'll act in the courtroom; the meekest lawyer can undergo a Jekyll and Hyde transformation.

Litigators are the most dynamic and abrasive subspecies in the legal trade. This isn't like dealing with a tax lawyer, where you have to get him to stop saying, "Well, that's a gray area."

Their drive is usually an asset. It can become a liability when you let them fly beyond radio range. You want to know what they're doing and why they're doing it (once in the courtroom it will be too late). Some customers recommend a choke collar.

The abrasiveness is often useful when dealing with underlings (that includes most bureaucrats). It can become a liability if they pointlessly abrade the wrong people. So keep an eye on them.

LOVE AFFAIRS USUALLY END SOMETIME

A fast, strange love affair is a very common working model for the customer-lawyer relationship. Fast, because it might last only one date, though two or three is more common. Strange, because you're there to do business, or should be—and the lawyer isn't in love with you, but with his client list.

In this scenario, the first date is a smashing success. The job gets done, and all the loose ends are tied up. (Lawyers are fond of tying up loose ends.)

The second date seems to drag a bit, but it gets done.

The third date seems to have trouble getting off the ground. Lawyer's out. Doesn't return your phone calls with that old enthusiasm. Can't seem to synchronize schedules.

It's over.

Sure, you can persist, and push this job through. If the lawyer is particularly competent, it may be worth it—because quality often returns after a couple more jobs.

Like a love affair, you may never know why it ended. You may not accept it at first. But in hindsight, you know *when* it ended. The glance that wasn't warm, the phone call that wasn't returned. It comes to the same thing; the thrill is gone.

MANIPULATION AND INTIMIDATION

The major training in manipulation and intimidation comes in law school, watching the teachers, and in conversations at the student bar—where the aspiring lawyers share tips on verbal methods, body language, what sort of suits to wear, and so on. The partners at law firms provide post-graduate training in setting up an impressive office, telephone technique, and pompous letter-writing. There really isn't that much difference between the informal training of a lawyer and an MBA; the lawyers just get more of it.

Manipulation and intimidation are primarily used by short-sighted people—people who focus on methods instead of goals, who see trees instead of forests. An active attempt to manipulate you should make you wonder if the lawyer's mind is on the job—and whether he's the right one for you.

Most types of intimidation are simply old (bad) habits which people never get around to eradicating. If you sense the intimidation is just an ingrained behavior pattern, and not too obnoxious, ignore it. Active attempts mean there is a personality clash on the way—the lawyer is not a workable employee.

MOTIVATION

These motivations are <u>not</u> in order of importance; lawyers are easy to stereotype, but they're hardly clones.

Power —No. Lawyers don't want power. They may think so when they enter law school, but by graduation decisiveness has been crippled by an endless loop tape recorder: "What if, but, on the other hand . . ." Complete autonomy makes them nervous. They want control—to be the indispensable chief advisor—but not king. If by accident they find themselves king, they'll spend their time in conferences instead of making decisions.

Status pleases them. They get some by being a lawyer. If you're important, then the lawyer gets a rise in status by association. If you're not important, there's not much mileage here; any other improvement in their status is going to cost you money.

Winning a case pleases the lawyers who like the courtroom scene, which is by no means the majority of lawyers. (This is more important to criminal lawyers, since civil trial lawyers often count settling on the courthouse steps as a win.)

Building the Client List. A rite of passage. This is one of the few business concepts they learn during law school (third year, at the student bar), and they develop a mighty fixation. Unfortunately, a client list is a concept unto itself. Lawyers don't automatically link it to the concept of repeat business. You have to gently make the connection for them.

Control is one of their main needs, but don't over-indulge them. If you have confidence in them, then give them responsibility for the legal strategies. But be firm; not a single inch over the line, into unwanted advice.

Stress. They seek it out, even when they don't really like it. Some customers say when they no longer associate you with excitement, you no longer get prompt service. There's truth there. But how much extra agitation do *you* need? Let this motivation lie.

Money is a much-overrated human motivation. I'd put it behind power, sex, recognition, and even the beaver-like American urge to build something. Still, it's one way to keep score. Since lawyers rarely have fun, or concrete results to admire, they count money and billable hours.

Many customers say lawyers are on a feeding frenzy, period—that money is their only reason for existence. I'll meet those customers half-way: many (or even most) lawyers are on a feeding frenzy, and some of them period.

Job survival (for associates)—which equals billable hours.

Showing off is important to a lawyer. It's often a useless motivation. Do we care if he wrote a great brief, or made a clause more complicated, or impressed another lawyer? Maybe—and maybe it just runs up the bill. Re-define success as *fulfilling your goal*. But don't make results all-or-nothing; people don't change overnight. Give him specific targets to hit along the way. Never say, "Call me when it's done."

A job well done. Certainly. But is it the job you want?

Respect for their ability is something lawyers appreciate, like anyone else. Their blindness to the customer's thoughts means they usually don't see it when it's there.

The customer's urgency. Urgency moves mountains. With amazing regularity, humans will respond to great need. But do lawyers respond? Yes and no. They can feel it; it stimulates them. But there is some strange chemistry going on; what starts as *your* urgency becomes not *their* urgency but, *theirs alone*. And so, an uncertain motivation.

The last four motivations are the most useful to a customer.

PROBLEM SOLVERS

Lawyers—by their own estimate—are problem solvers. In the last two decades, what with all the chatter of problems, solutions, issues, and challenges, it's understandable that people would forget what this means: *a problem-solver needs problems.* And if you don't provide one, he'll probably go looking.

Is this semantics? I don't think so—in fact, let me ask: Has anyone seen a genuine opportunity lately? Something that is fundamentally beneficial?

I had one, some years ago—the opportunity to buy a building cheaply. The beast was slippery, and I barely lassoed it long enough to take it by the lawyer's office, where I asked him to see if it had fleas—a limited request, which he must not have heard, for in no time he had determined that it was not an opportunity, but a problem, and wanted to keep it under observation for two days, so that a solution could be devised.

Knowing that the creature would escape during the two day observation period, I simply paid the owner and took it home, where I found it did indeed have fleas; but with a series of scrubbings it regained its full health and served me well for many years.

PROCRASTINATION

Is taught in law school. The professors let the students know that finishing assignments in the eleventh hour is inevitable, given the majestic complexity of the law. "Inevitable" quickly comes to mean "acceptable."

Ten years later these students are down at the courthouse, telling the judge, ". . . it's not my fault, can I get an extension on that filing?"

You aren't getting paid to revamp your lawyer's efficiency. But you do want to know things are getting done on time. So get the hard dates, make a timetable, and keep the lawyer on it.

Keep yourself on the timetable too. Legal work is as boring as it is frustrating.

Procrastination fits in nicely with HYSTERIA (p.13) and CRISIS MANAGEMENT (p.58). It's minimized by PROJECT MANAGEMENT (p.85).

(Most lawyers keep detailed calendars. So how can they procrastinate? Because they either schedule early, and then ignore the calendar—or more reckless, when something needs to be done <u>by</u> the 30th, they schedule it <u>for</u> the 30th.)

WHAT LAWYERS RESPECT

Lawyers respect:

- Intelligence, but their view of intelligence is narrow: basically, what comes out of your mouth. Articulation, debate, logic, vocabulary. The actual quality of your judgment isn't critical, as long as you're not an outright lunatic; it's your neck at risk, not theirs.

- The ability to control other people (preferably not including them).

- Large quantities of money.

- "Winners."

- Legal knowledge (preferably less than theirs).

ADOPT AN ATTITUDE

This book combines two approaches to lawyers: the business attitude and the autocratic attitude. I favor the pure business attitude—but personalities usually enter the field, and that's where the autocratic attitude can come into play.

THE BUSINESS ATTITUDE

A pure business attitude—or as close as possible—is the right method for most customers. It focuses on results, and avoids personalities. This is a world view, not an opinion; it's not open to discussion by the lawyer. Here is the frame of mind:

- I'm buying a service which provides the following results: _____(insert laundry list)_____. (Obviously an experienced customer will be more specific, but everyone has some idea of what they want.)

- I need to know what results can be expected, how much it will cost, and when it can be done. This information is necessary to my decision. Without this information I can't make any decision. If I can't make a decision I'll have to let this job drop. (And then you will not be hired.)

- If the value (to me) of the results is greater than the cost, *and* the cost is within my budget, I'll buy.

- If the value of the results is less than the cost, *or* the cost exceeds my budget, I won't buy.

- It's a business decision, you understand. (Actually, the lawyer may not understand, but ignore that. The important thing is that he's met businesslike customers before. This won't be a new experience.)

This attitude is essentially the practice of PROJECT MANAGEMENT (p.85). You ignore any negative aspects of the lawyer's personality. Once beyond basic manners, there is no reality but results and cost; results and cost are the only meaning in the universe. In the end all conversations return to results and cost.

Since results and cost are the only realities, it doesn't matter whether the lawyer thinks you are "right," or thinks you're acting rationally. If he starts debating, you want to determine how the point relates to results and cost. If he wanders too far, you have to reintroduce your original purpose. (Some lawyers claim debating is a means of examining problems . . . I've heard many debates, with many ideas laid in the grave, but I've rarely seen an idea emerge in good health.)

Like a terrier digging for a bone, there is only one goal—yours—and you ignore all distractions.

The business attitude is also useful if you wrap up the job a lot sooner than the lawyer expected. You tell him you'll be "giving up this approach," that you "don't feel the results will justify the time spent." Suspecting they are being fired, most lawyers will try to argue you out of your decision. Go past this argument with the same steady business attitude. You're offering them a chance to save face; most will take the opportunity. Firing is much more relaxed when it stays in the realm of ideas and results. Just as final, though.

THE AUTOCRATIC ATTITUDE

Outwardly focuses on results (and the results *are* important). At a lower level it focuses on personalities. Power dynamics. Pecking orders. Big monkey and little monkey.

I met Bill Friedman at a barbecue. The host—heading off to turn the roast—said, "Bill knows more than I do. He's been in charge of a bunch of federal regulatory lawyers for years." Bill had the look of a man who knows his mind, so I went right to the point:

"Pleased to meet you. Do you happen to have a coherent ten-point theory on controlling lawyers?"

"Absolutely!" he answered, and here it is (in fact, he only gave me five points, but they're good ones):

The Bill Friedman Method

- Be autocratic.

  autocracy, *n.* 1. unlimited authority over others, invested in a single person
  [Author's Note: Bill later mentioned that he didn't mean the customer should be nasty. Agreed: most people with real authority have fairly good manners. Autocrats don't need to abuse people; they're above that.]

- Communicate the following ideas to the lawyer:
  You're a hired advisor.
  Your purpose is to advance what I believe or need.
  If you can't do that, you can't serve me.

- It's OK to play golf with them, but only at your own club.
  [I assume that Bill also meant ". . . and not too often."]

- Get on top and never let them up.

- Bill added that—like military people—lawyers live by rigid social rules, and people accustomed to such rules are prepared to take orders.

The autocratic method works best for those who know what they want—and think they have a divine right to command. Bill Friedman was a U.S. Army officer for some 20 years, a pretty good way to develop the attitude. J. P. Morgan must have had the same attitude, judging by his comment, "I pay lawyers to do what I tell them, not to tell me what I can't do." But if you don't have it, stick with the business approach.

THE DEMOCRATIC ATTITUDE

You won't find modern theories of management in this book. There is no participative management, no profit sharing, and no quality circles. With good reason: lawyers are not regular employees, for whom you're responsible. They are temporary employees who earn good money, better than most of their customers, and who usually reckon they're more important than the customers.

Responsibility aside, democracy doesn't work. Lawyers are ferociously class-conscious. You can get on top and stay there, with the autocratic attitude, or you can refuse to play games, with the business attitude. That's about it.

ADVICE, UNSOLICITED

Don't show the lawyer a "Whatever you say" attitude. Focus on the specific suggestions, and make the decision yourself. You don't want him to start feeling too free with advice. Facts first, then advice—if you ask for it. Then you decide.

Sometimes you don't notice—until about the third suggestion—that advice is being rammed down your throat. It's not too late to clarify your attitude. If he continues to get aggressive with advice, tell him that you'll have to think about it. If you decide to take it, call back and tell him to go ahead. Make him wait.

Immature? A waste of valuable time? Perhaps, but it sets the ground rules; those who know enough to offer advice should know enough to be tactful.

Some types of advice should never be allowed: don't let a lawyer advise you on your life or personal affairs. That isn't what you're paying for. You want to know what your legal situation is, and then have specific jobs carried out.

You should be no more interested in a lawyer's personal advice than a new plumber's advice on bathroom decor. *If* the plumber gets to know you, and you come to respect the plumber's artistic sense, then maybe you'd ask which type of faucet handles would look best on the shower.

Ditto the lawyer.

See FAMILIARITY *(p.43)*.

BE RATIONAL BUT NOT TRANSPARENT

Be passably rational, so a lawyer can tell when you're serious about something. You don't want to call from jail and have him think you're just being hysterical again.

But don't feel obliged to explain your thinking. You're the boss; you don't have to. Unless there's a good rapport, you want the lawyer to know the goal, and that's all you want.

The more sensitive customers will want to share their hopes and fears. This is usually a mistake. To explain your reasoning is usually to be ignored, and at worst, to wind up debating with the lawyer. *Never* debate with a lawyer. There's no way to win; when aroused to argument, a lawyer will always want the last say.

CONSUMERISM, BELLIGERENT

Charging in aggressively (waving a five-page contract from the back of a consumer advocate book) will accomplish two things: it will annoy the lawyer—and tell him you're naive.

See CONTRACTS *(p.120)*.

CONTROL, LOSS OF

If you deal with lawyers on any sort of regular basis, you'll sooner or later lose control of a relationship. If you feel badly about this, just purge your guilt by saying, "Damn, I've ruined a perfectly usable lawyer!"

A lawyer out of control will predictably resent being put back into the passenger seat. You can do it, sometimes, but it may take years to re-establish the right relationship.

If it's between jobs, replacement is usually the best course.

DELIVERY BOY, WHO'S GOING TO BE

If your lawyer is having difficulty treating you with respect, don't make it worse by acting as a delivery boy. At that point, conferences are about the only reason you should travel to the lawyer's office. (When big business hires lawyers, the lawyers trot over to the business and make a presentation. The "beauty parade," some lawyers call it.)

If necessary use delivery services, overnight mail services, fax, and telephone. It costs a bit, but if you play delivery boy for a disrespectful lawyer, what will it cost you in the long run?

DRESSING TO IMPRESS A LAWYER

If you normally wear a suit, that's fine. If you occasionally wear a suit, it can't hurt to let the lawyer know that.

If you're a farmer, think twice before wearing the Sunday suit. Employees should never develop the idea that you're trying to impress them.

FAMILIARITY

Premature familiarity breeds contempt.

You don't have to be pompous or unpleasant. Just don't be personal right away.

The time to accept familiarity is *after* you get respect—whether that takes one minute or five years. It depends on you and the lawyer.

There can be exceptions to the rule. If your situation is really unfortunate, familiarity may simply mean the lawyer is sympathetic.

FEARS OF CUSTOMERS

It's common enough for customers to be intimidated by their lawyer. The best solution is to never hire a lawyer who intimidates you, but perhaps you were in a hurry. If you're stuck with an overbearing lawyer, try this:

Write out what you want before each conversation. Think of it as a shopping list—and a script. When you meet, go down the list point by point. Put a check mark next to each one.

DON'T DEBATE. If he starts giving orders, write them down. (If the orders don't suit your plans, you can always make a paper airplane out of the sheet of paper.) Once he's finished that, then say, "OK, and now I have a couple more points to clear up. You mentioned earlier . . ." (This may drive him crazy, but that's fine—it means the list has taken charge of the conference.)

If the lawyer cuts you off, you may have to let him go before the job gets done. If the lawyer snarls at you—well, customers with money and experience seem to have some standard responses:

1. Stand up and walk out without a word.

2. Stand up, say "Send me the bill," and walk out.

3. Run all over the lawyer.

The first response is perfectly good style. I would never use #2; it's a great line, but paying off a useless employee in full is a luxury I can't afford.

IF YOU'RE SERIOUS, LET THE LAWYER KNOW

Lawyers see a lot of conflict. So they see a lot of emotional customers, particularly angry and vindictive ones. This doesn't mean they take every agitated customer seriously; far from it. But it's what they're accustomed to; at least they know the customer has motivation. When a customer doesn't even look tense, they'll have that much more trouble taking the job seriously.

If you're the reserved, soft-spoken type, the lawyer may be wondering what you really want. So make sure he understands the goal, and give him a solid clue that you're serious.

(Experienced criminals and business people are assumed to be serious, if not poison mean. So this chapter doesn't apply to them.)

IMAGE, WHAT DO YOU WANT YOURS TO BE?

People will definitely judge you by your employees.

So how will they judge you after meeting your lawyer?

(If you're involved in a civil court case, you'll probably be hiring a litigator. Most attack lawyers are short on manners. Be prepared to live with a bit of aggravation.)

THANK YOU

It's easy to feel ungrateful when you were billed $100 per hour.

Nevertheless. The kind of lawyer you <u>should</u> be hiring—a human being—is going to appreciate thanks. Remember, the lawyer believes (or half-way believes) that his time is worth that much. Maybe it is, maybe it isn't, but the belief is there. If you got good service, ignore the hourly rate and say thank you.

TRUST

Trust <u>is not</u> a substitute for understanding the situation.

Trust <u>is</u> reassurance. When you don't have the time or energy to review everything, you can still sleep.

At a more fundamental level, trust is central. Good people do better work for those who trust them. And it's much more pleasant doing business with someone of integrity.

Basics

ADVERSARY SYSTEM, THE

The adversary system was supposed to make everyone work hard to present his side of the question (as contrasted with some other legal systems, where the judge asks the questions, decides, and that's it). In the adversary system the opposing lawyers would each present their version of reality, and out of this porridge of truth and lies would come truth.

It didn't work all that well. Instead of achieving consistent truth, the adversary system has achieved irregular truth and corrupted society's values in the process. Today the adversary system operates under one of the strangest theories in the known universe.

> "If they're losing, we must be winning."

If you want to hear a sane voice, you may have to talk to yourself.

(The adversary mentality, in which lawyers play "advocate," makes it almost impossible to focus lawyers' minds on cooperative enterprises. They can't really grasp that sometimes the pie is so large it doesn't matter how accurately you slice it; everybody gets a good slice. A lawyer will be incredibly reluctant to work *for the deal*; he'll want to work for *you*, and keep hacking at the pie until it's ruined for everyone.)

AVOIDING LITIGATION

"May you have a lawsuit in which you know you are in the right."
                                                    Gypsy curse

The public has been warned that lawsuits benefit lawyers more than customers, but there will be suits as long as there are corrupt individuals and organizations, vengeful customers, free-loaders who make a living by suing their fellow humans—and lawyers, of course (with extra time on their hands, a love of problems, a hired gun attitude, and the belief that the most advantageous place to settle disputes is on the courthouse steps).

The best general defense against litigation is to not get involved with unethical people. This works well, though it tends to cut down on your circle of acquaintances. But it can't eliminate suits; humans being what they are, they sometimes enter your life without an invitation, either filing suit against you, or pushing you beyond reasonable bounds, to the point that you file a suit against them.

Nevertheless, try to look at your long-term interests. Maybe it would be better to drop the suit, or settle, and use the money you would have spent on lawyers for something more satisfying. The last time I was tempted to file an unproductive suit (against a corrupt bureaucracy), I chose an alternative tactic: I sent a contribution to an effective citizens group which was (and is) bitterly opposing that particular bureaucracy. The public will benefit, and I sleep easy knowing that the bureaucrats are suffering endlessly for their crimes—all for much less than the cost of a lawyer.

There is another, more specific, strategy to reduce suits against you. No, not ethical behavior; that won't do you much good in court. But closely linked to ethics, there is a policy that can help reduce suits in all sorts of relationships: *Say what you mean, do what you say—and keep evidence of both.* Many frivolous lawsuits will fade when a chiseler's lawyer finds that you followed this policy all the way to the practice of keeping notes. The chiseler may still want to sue, or try to extort a settlement, but the disenchanted lawyer, seeing failure on the horizon, may ask for a $10,000 advance payment . . . and chiselers don't like spending.

Some Anti-Litigation Tactics

- Arbitration can work. The strength of arbitration lies in saving face and money, not justice (though justice frequently emerges from an arbitrator's office). Since you may have to suggest arbitration, don't act too eager; this needs to be presented as an "everyone yields a bit" situation (bitter pills are easiest swallowed in company).

- Keep lawyers out of good relationships. Selling an extra acre of land to your mother-in-law is not the place to be trotting in an unknown and uncontrolled lawyer.

- Shoot for the gun hand. Go after the opposition lawyers. Is the suit against you frivolous? Federal courts have rules on frivolous suits; lawyers have been fined on occasion for trotting in suits that "have no merit," which includes "for purposes of harassment." Many state courts have comparable rules.

  Your lawyers may be reluctant to turn their guns on their brethren. Likewise a judge may be uncomfortable—but if the rules are there, he should at least go through the paces. And then, some judges are genuinely tired of frivolous and parasitic lawsuits.

- Suing a bureaucracy, either a big corporation or the government? Has a lower manager kicked the original problem "over to legal" in order to cover his ass? Will "legal" then go to the mat—because that's where the fun is—figuring a loss can be blamed on the judge or jury?

  Does the upper management know what's happening? Upper management is more likely to put on the thinking cap; they may not want to go to court. It could be worthwhile to write a letter, letting them know: A. They can still fix the problem without losing face. B. You will play hardball if they don't fix the problem.

Of course, upper management has no monopoly on intelligence or ethics; there's no guarantee that writing the president will generate justice. The CEO or directors may stonewall on one of several theories: "The stockholders will be angry if the company makes good on this claim." / "I'll be changing jobs soon, then it'll be someone else's problem." / "If we delay paying off, that money will earn good interest in the meantime." / "The corporation is rich and immortal; the plaintiff may run out of money to pay his lawyers, or lose hope, or die."

- Can you find a solution that satisfies everyone? Is there a way everyone can save face and avoid financial loss? E.g. The developers who promised you a house and then sold it to someone else . . . do they have another house around the corner, which would suit you better? Will they give you a discount on that one to cool you off—while still making some profit themselves?

- Fight fire with gasoline. Can you interest a government agency in this matter, bringing plague and pestilence upon the land in the form of inspectors, investigators, and eager young government lawyers? (This could be more grief than you want.)

Notions That Lead on to Court

—"They'll settle because they can't stand the publicity this case will generate." What publicity? Over 50% of the news is spoon-fed to the media by publicists, spokesmen, and promoters. Publicity can be lethal, but you'll have to make it. If it's an individual, they may not care at all about publicity.

—"It's just business to them. They'll settle because it's cheaper." Maybe. An organization being sued may look at the long picture. They want to discourage suits; show them a crazy claim with lots of publicity, and they'll probably go to the mat.

—"They'd rather settle for $10,000 than pay their lawyers $20,000." Maybe, maybe . . .

BACKUPS

If you need a lawyer often, keep a backup in mind at all times. It would be hard to overemphasize the importance of this. A backup is choice, it is alternative, it is option.

(While shopping you'll collect the names of some extra possibilities; save the names.)

That's common sense. There's a more fundamental reason: With an alternative, you aren't trapped, and so you think more clearly. You act more intelligently.

Furthermore, a backup puts the customer in the strongest possible negotiating position, knowing: "I don't need this person's service; there is a substitute around the corner." To a customer who is not aggressive—or even assertive—this added confidence is even more important. It shows on your face, and can make a difference in the lawyer's attitude.

When You Don't Need a Backup

You have complete confidence in your lawyer—and at least one of his partners or associates. (Your lawyer might be on vacation when you need him.)

BUREAUCRACY

Is out there, waiting to torment you. To do business with a lawyer is to deal with law. Law is a government monopoly. To deal with the government is to be inconvenienced, at best. A good lawyer can reduce but not eliminate this.

Try to discriminate between the nuisances generated by the lawyer and those generated by the legal system. Many legal procedures have delays built in by law. The bureaucracies surrounding the courts can take additional weeks or months to do their job, and the courts can take years just to reach trial.

Most of the bureaucratic delays and aggravations will be laid out at the beginning, when you are sitting in the lawyer's office asking, "Right. Then what's the next step? OK, when does that happen?" (See PROJECT MANAGEMENT on timelines, p.85.)

Delays that pop up later should make you wonder. Bureaucracies are glacial, but their level of sloth is usually predictable. Courts can be more frivolous; a trial date may indeed be shifted with hardly any warning.

In either case, you can try to match the lawyer's explanation to your timeline and see if it's plausible—or head on down to the courthouse to see what papers have been filed, what the judges and bureaucracy have been up to.

COMMON SENSE SOLUTION
(IN PLACE OF A LEGAL ONE)

If a lawyer offers a common-sense solution: Take it! And pay the bill with thanks. This is the best of all worlds.

Common sense is not necessarily the lawyer who says, "This isn't really a legal matter," or "You can't win. Why don't you let it go?" Quite a few lawyers can do that when they don't want the job.

The peak of common sense is the lawyer who can ignore a good profit, and say, "Have you considered telephoning . . . and saying . . .", or "Do you think it might work if you drive over to . . . and . . ." Yes, it's unsolicited advice—but at this point it's from a human being.

(I found common sense in the first legal encounter of my life, when I paid a lawyer $50 to look at a lease and tell me, "Well, I'm afraid it means what it says—your lease is up this year. But why do you want to keep this place? Rents have dropped in that area, and you could rent a better building for less money." In other words, check the classified ads.)

CONSULTATION

A lawyer's most valuable service is getting you out of jail.

The second most valuable service is consultation. Hardly anyone gets through life without a situation where they need legal knowledge. It keeps you out of trouble; occasionally it shows an opportunity. Dollar for dollar, minute for minute, consultation is the best buy a lawyer can offer.

Lawyers are well accustomed to customers calling with a quick question; when the customer wants to understand the big picture, they become confused. Most of them would rather give fifteen minutes worth of useless half-answer than charge an hour for a complete answer. You see the same kind of thinking in other businesses—but it certainly runs against the saying that "Advice is a lawyer's stock in trade."

Make it clear what you want when you make the appointment. Prepare him. Try calling it "risk analysis." Let him know that it's more than a quick question—he'll have to do some explanation—but it's not the beginning of a long and expensive relationship. Otherwise he'll feel a compulsion to take charge of the interview (and scribble on legal pads)—instead of thoughtfully answering your questions.

If he can't seem to get the idea, try another lawyer. Often you never do get an answer—you end up calling several and then piecing together an answer from the various opinions.

Some of the best consultations I've gotten have been while lawyers were giving lectures—or directly afterward, when I peppered them with questions. A lecture is a very different situation from an office consultation; lawyers have very little fear of malpractice, or any economic motive to withhold the hard facts. It's also different from a cocktail party conversation; they're on stage, and they know the audience is impressed by hard-hitting facts, not mush. Make the most of lectures. But don't think you have finally found a decisive lawyer; when you call him at his office, he could go right back to talking about "gray areas" and "tailoring a solution to your needs."

COURTESY FROM THE LAWYER

Courtesy isn't one of a lawyer's job skills. (Though since the trade still pretends to be a gentlemen's club, they'll avoid most of the gross social blunders.)

The most important part, though, isn't whether they're courteous to you; it's how they represent you. If you want them to be courteous with others, tell them so.

(An over-aggressive lawyer can ruin your future relationships.)

See LETTERS FROM THE LAWYER'S DESK (*p.78*).

CRISIS MANAGEMENT

The last stop in uncontrolled PROCRASTINATION (p.31). There is, however, a difference between the two. Procrastination is a miserable way of life, but it won't directly produce disaster, unless you miss an important deadline.

Crisis management is a more dynamic type of folly. This is where bad decisions are made—and acted on, before you catch them.

Crisis management is minimized by PROJECT MANAGEMENT (p.85).

CUSTOM WORK—IS IT?

Lawyers want the public to think standardized solutions are dangerous. They can be—but several million houses trade hands every year with standardized contracts. Both buyer and seller are usually cheated somewhere in the transaction, but the results are rarely disastrous.

Though a third party actively butting into your business can complicate any job (and increase costs), it doesn't necessarily make the job unique. The truth is that very few solutions are custom-built by lawyers. *Semi*-custom is the reality.

In jobs where there is no third party, the lawyer pulls something out of his files or out of a law book and makes a few changes, or calls a friend for advice, and copies his wording. Lawyers will say there are no standard solutions. In a sense, that's true; for example, the loose-leaf contract books on my shelf generally offer several sample contracts for each type of job (along with a discussion of the pros and cons).

There's nothing wrong with this; it's half-way efficient. It's when lawyers charge for useless customizing (or custom prices for semi-custom work) that it becomes dishonest. This is the sales talk of "tailoring the contract to your needs."

This isn't rocket science. You're not going to the moon. If you're like me, you can't afford perfection. Just reasonable safety.

A rule of thumb: *A lawyer who really has to build it from scratch must not know much about the job.*

DEAL KILLERS

Absolutely true. It isn't that the lawyers are actually trying to kill the deal. They just want to address the possibilities, protect your interests, dot the "i"s, cross the "t"s—and be a central part of the decision process, instead of a consultant. And they love to "one-up" the other party's lawyers; in this game, being the last one to add a clause gains them great face.

KILLING A DEAL

Lawyers want to represent your interests in person right from the beginning of the deal. This may chase away the other party in the deal, sometimes for the simple reason that he doesn't want to pay his own lawyer to review your lawyer's bag of tricks.

Usually the other party won't run for the hills at the first sighting of your lawyer. However, the actual contract may get him moving, especially if you let your lawyer "fully protect your interests" with a page of "shalls" and "heretofores." Extended contracts can scare the inexperienced, and often annoy the experienced.

The over-aggressive contract approaches a more certain doom when the other party pays his own lawyer some good money to come up with a counter-offer that he hopes will satisfy you—and your lawyer shoots it down.

Another round of counter-offers, stipulations, clauses, nickels, and dimes, and the deal is dead. Friends who practice law in Canada have commented that "The American lawyers do seem to try and squeeze every drop out of a deal."

Great, you say! But how long do you expect the other party to hang around? Are you dealing with someone from the Mediterranean, who might haggle all year for the pleasure—or an American, who has other business needing attention?

An hour later the other party is whacking a ball down the golf course asking himself, "Why did I ever try to do business with that idiot?"

Prevention

- Know what you want from the deal.

- Make a distinction between protecting yourself—and asking the other guy to put his head in the guillotine. (Only the devil writes <u>perfect</u> contracts—and even he gets tricked sometimes.)

- Decide what you can expect to get—or get away with. Your lawyer assumes the other fellow is an illiterate cretin. Is he? Will he miss the significance of clause #23? Where he is promising to "pay on your behalf" for virtually any lawsuit that might be brought against you, including ones that have almost nothing to do with the deal?

- You should understand your own contract. That usually means paying your own lawyer to explain the legal implications of anything you don't understand. That's the way it is.

- Consider avoiding on-going contracts entirely. If the nature of a relationship is really a series of individual transactions, you might want to leave it that way, instead of making an agreement that could require you to do your part—even if the other party doesn't do his.

To some business people prevention means never allowing their own lawyer to talk to someone else's without supervision—the goal is to keep the lawyers from arguing back and forth until the contract is ten pages long and the deal is dead. Other business people don't let their lawyers talk to the opposition lawyers at all, but this can lead to other problems; until they talk to your lawyer, the opposition lawyers (who may be in control of their own customer) can persist in thinking they can demand anything, as though you were illiterate. In fact, keeping the lawyers apart can lead to the worst of all scenarios, in which you find yourself an errand boy for both lawyers: their lawyer tells you the sky is green, you go back to your lawyer, who tells you the sky is blue, then back to their lawyer, who says he meant the sky is green just on Thursdays, and on and on . . . Nip this one in the bud; don't treat the opposition lawyers as equals unless they have authority to act.

And see FIRST USE, NO *(p.69).*

DEAL MAKERS?

Sometimes. Though lawyers rarely create a deal, they can often negotiate better than an inexperienced customer can:

- Within their own specialty (business, real estate, divorce, etc.), lawyers have a head packed with knowledge on what is considered acceptable and what isn't. Terms, clauses, financing arrangements.

- They're often meaner than the customers.

- They're sometimes more skilled in the tactics of deal making, such as juggling numbers to reduce the tax man's cut, taking opposing lawyers out for expensive lunches, or getting busybodies out of the way by creating useless errands.

Even the experienced may feel they need to trot in a lawyer:

- When would-be "sharks" just can't get it through their heads that you understand the situation as well as they do. Perversely, these sharks often assume that a lawyer knows it all.

- To torment the competition and wear them down.

The lawyers who see themselves as "transaction lawyers" will place the most emphasis on making a deal. When they are being paid a percentage of the closing price, instead of by the hour, they develop an even greater interest in making the deal. This is a pleasant reversal from the image of deal killers, but there is one new hitch: like real estate agents, the lawyers may focus on closing the deal at the expense of making a good deal for their customer. If a business sells for $8 million (at a straight 2% commission), instead of the $10 million asking price, a lawyer could still collect $160,000. That's not as good as $200,000, but it's better than $0, which is what the lawyer will get if the business doesn't sell.

And Three Functions to Any Hired Negotiator

- Having a "front man" helps keep your cards covered, if that's what you want.

- A hired negotiator isn't emotionally involved.

- The competition is more likely to speak freely to a hired negotiator than a principal. (Though not necessarily more honestly.)

But when someone wants me to talk to their lawyer, I ask myself some questions: "Why am I talking to someone who doesn't have the authority to sign on the dotted line? Shouldn't I be speaking to the decision-maker? If the decision-maker is too busy to talk to me . . . are there any alternatives? Would this time be better spent looking for a person or company who is more eager? If there's no acceptable alternative, shouldn't I call the decision-maker directly?"

Your own lawyer will almost always advise you not to call the principals directly. There may be a valid reason: perhaps you or the other principal are short-tempered, or perhaps the other principal will think you're weakening. Usually, however, your lawyer can't—or won't—explain his reasoning.

Talking to someone's hired negotiator—particularly a lawyer—always makes me weary; after all, I could be doing something productive, like taking a stroll in the park.

DESCRIBING PROBLEMS

The law contains fine lines and traps. How many? A rule of thumb would be: people who know nothing of law underestimate the traps, and people who know a little bit overestimate them. In either case, the world's most decisive lawyer may still need the finicky details.

Put the facts on paper. Do it before office visits, do it before phone calls. You'll use less of the lawyer's time, it's cheaper, you'll be less likely to miss something.

There is an additional, less obvious reason—the lawyer is likely to re-define the situation in his own terms. Without a list of facts and questions, you can be side-tracked.

DOCUMENTS AND EVIDENCE

Lawyers usually want all the pertinent paperwork. Reasonable enough, but you might fire the lawyer—and your papers may become hostages.

Unless necessary, always give your lawyer copies instead of originals. Get copies of everything the lawyer produces. Have him mail you copies automatically. There is no need to be aggressive—lawyers are used to sending copies. They think it keeps the customers happy. (It often does.)

FAST STARTS (THAT FIZZLE?)

Fast starts are a common ailment in overeager or overstressed lawyers. You call a new lawyer and tell him your problem. He says there's no time to waste, and suggests you come to his office the same day. You drive on down and have a chat.

Scenario One: You leave an hour later knowing that the lawyer was right, there's no time to waste—and knowing the two of you have agreed on a tight plan of action, which he is already carrying out.

Scenario Two: is far more likely. After a very boring and unproductive hour you leave wondering "What, exactly, is the plan of action? And what's the hurry?" You're probably looking at a quick fizzle. He may never even call you back.

If the lawyer is still agitated during the office visit—but still doesn't offer a coherent plan of action—then be prepared for a slow fizzle. Typically there will be a couple of adrenalized phone calls over the next day, and then he sputters out.

Fizzles can be useful when you just want a quick (albeit hazy) analysis. Especially since they tend to fade away without ever generating a bill.

Summary: When a new and unknown lawyer seems to be agitated out of proportion to the situation, give a bit of thought to alternative lawyers.

See HYSTERIA *(p.13) and* MOTIVATION *(p.28).*

FILING THE PAPERWORK

Keeping papers is part of managing the project; part of managing your lawyer; and definitely part of firing him. You need a complete file to get rolling with a new lawyer, and you can't be certain of getting everything back from your ex-lawyer.

Copy everything. Keep everything. Even if you just stuff it in boxes. (In fact, that's a fairly efficient way to file the many papers that will never be read again.)

See DOCUMENTS AND EVIDENCE *(p.65)*.

FIRST USE

First Use is when you roll your lawyer into view before the other person.

The appearance of a lawyer has varying effects on people. To some it's business as usual. To others it resembles a nuclear missile appearing over the horizon; they may react abruptly.

Regardless of effect, everyone is aware that you have brought a lawyer into the picture.

FIRST USE, NO

First Use is usually foolish when opportunity is knocking—even when you foresee problems. These are the times to keep the lawyers out of sight.

Examples:

- The beginning of anything promising—car, house, business deal, adoption, whatever. If the money or consequences are serious, then *do* ask a lawyer to lay out the legal situation, or work out the ideal contract. Do it before you make any promises—written *or* oral. But do it in private.

- When doing business with family and friends, never let a lawyer "represent your interests." Not if you want to stay on good terms with the family, or keep your friends. You may need a simple contract, in case one of you gets hit by a bus, but no more than that. If you can't trust someone close to you, *don't do business with them.*

Specific Exceptions:

- You're playing out of your league, and the sharks know it. The appearance of a knowledgeable lawyer frequently calms the feeding frenzy. (Bring in a rookie, though, and the sharks will close for the kill.)

- You want big concessions, and you're willing to risk killing the deal. (If you want reasonable concessions, just say so. If you're someone who loves that last little bit of horse-trading, then bring the lawyer in later. Some people take offense at renegotiation, though.)

- You're dealing with someone who is much too impressed by his own cunning. The presence of an authority figure may sober him up.

FIRST USE, YES

If you're unhappy with the way things are going.

For example, you want to kill a deal. This doesn't mean a lawyer can get you out of any contract; if you made the wrong agreement, you may be stuck with either a bad deal or a losing lawsuit. But in many instances, anyone who is serious about business will seriously reconsider doing business with *you*—after a few torturous rounds with your lawyer.

Likewise, First Use makes sense when you are dealing with the type of business that routinely cheats its customers. Consistently dishonest businesses usually take a "win a few, lose a few" attitude. In predicaments like this, letters from aggressive lawyers can be a fast, cheap solution—one of the company's supervisors will probably "review" the situation, and often finds that the lower echelon "misunderstood." Making an insurance claim is the classic example of this usage.

Or in a similar vein, when dealing with people who are bad apples, but not quite rotten. If these mealy apples know what they ought to be doing, but don't quite have the motivation—that extra little bit of expert power may help them see the light. Some years ago a friend lent money to a couple of rock promoters, who failed to promote rock, and neglected to repay the money. After much wasted badgering my friend hired a lawyer, one of the relaxed types, subspecies "old sage." The lawyer said he would give the impresarios a call; the next day he called my friend back and said:

"Well, they brought the money over."

"How much?" howled my friend.

"Oh, all of it."

"What did you say?" my friend asked.

"Oh, we did a little horse-trading . . ."

And there is another, less aggressive type of First Use: showing people that you have a lawyer, just like they do (sort of like showing them you can afford a gold watch).

GOBBLEDYGOOK

Is unacceptable. You should understand at least 95% of what the lawyer is saying. (Some good lawyers have told me I should understand 100%—but I rarely do.)

Otherwise, how do you know the lawyer is discussing the same situation? How do you know what he intends to do? How do you know he even understands you? Don't try to reform a lawyer whom you can't understand. Just don't hire him.

Conversely, don't reject a lawyer because you *can* understand him. In a perverse sort of logic, many customers tell themselves that a lawyer who makes it all too simple can't really know what he's doing*—so they go find themselves a lawyer who spouts mumbo-jumbo. Those customers will pay heavily for their strange sense of priorities.

The most bizarre form of gobbledygook comes from the lawyer who has the gall to tell you that it's too complicated to explain. A lawyer might not use those exact words; my favorite memory is a lawyer who told me—when I pointedly asked how a mortgage release would be handled—"We have ways of handling that." As a friend commented later, "Oh, you mean 'don't worry your little head about that!'" Since it wasn't my lawyer, and it wasn't going to be my problem, I let it drop after three tries—and was not surprised when the buyer had difficulty refinancing the property. (Persistence is important, though; the unhappy buyer and I straightened out the mess the next time I was in town, two years later.)

*Thomas Edison knew better: "Simplicity is the essence of genius."

HOW TO REDUCE PRODUCTIVITY

Ever fertile, the human mind has created infinite ways to reduce productivity. Here are a few of the most common:

Interfering

- Call daily to check up. This will waste the lawyer's time, and help him lose track of the goal.

- Change your mind regularly. Re-define the purpose of the job. Eventually this will un-define the job.

Killing Motivation

- Bring the lawyer another job before the first one is finished. He'll work on whichever seems more urgent, which is fine—and move the other one from the front of the line to the back of the line, which is not fine.

  In a further possibility, he may bounce back and forth between the two jobs, without ever grabbing hold of one and finishing it.

  (Multiple jobs also make it hard to decipher the bill. Lawyers know this and often use it to their advantage.)

- Be nice. That way the lawyer will push your work to the back burner if he is short of time. Later, when the crisis approaches, and you begin to press, he'll resent you for being pushy.

  (Meanwhile, the tough-but-fair customer will have his job done, and have called to say thanks, whereupon the lawyer will remember that "He wants results, you know it, must be a winner . . . but he's really pretty nice once you get to know him.")

- Make full payment in advance. Would you give your dog a biscuit *before* the trick? Humans, possessing the concept of obligation, are sometimes motivated by advance payment—but the odds aren't good. Advance payment is far more likely to kill motivation.

- Over-supervise. This book advises you to take charge—to supervise. But *over*-supervising can be harmful. What's the difference?

Over-supervising means robbing someone of his sense of responsibility. Timelines are a good example. If a lawyer knows you have orchestrated the job on paper, his sense of responsibility fades; why worry, when someone else is already worried? So make a timeline—that's good supervision. But don't let the lawyer know you have it—that's over-supervision. Let him think you have a photographic memory; this will keep him on his toes.

A human's sense of responsibility can be stolen in a moment, but it takes months to restore. Usually there's no time. The customer is forced to turn to the only quick substitute—pressure. At that point the customer has found a new job—full-time supervisor.

JARGON AND KEY PHRASES

Jargon

Professional courtesy means obliging another lawyer, e.g. agreeing to postpone a court date because the opposition lawyer had something urgent come up; or isn't prepared; or has to do lunch that day. Every trade has give and take; it greases the wheels, and sometimes both business owner and customer come out ahead. Lawyers take it too far. It's *usually* not damaging. On the other hand, the lawyer rarely tells the customer what he's done. Then it is dishonest.

To analyze —to read and dissect; also to get a quick education at the customer's expense.

To review —to read and generally consider; also to get a quick education at the customer's expense.

Research —can be an expensive word. You need to know how much research. You need to wonder if anyone else in town already has the answer in his head.

A case —a court case, to most lawyers, or something heading in that direction. If you weren't expecting to go to court, this word should get your attention; you need to know what the lawyer is thinking.

Expanding the work —over-lawyering; running the meter.

Client management —controlling the client, or his bank account.

Phrases

". . . tailor it to your situation . . ."
- *We've never done this before, but we're willing to learn, at full hourly rates.*
- *We want to charge you a custom price for a semi-custom job.*

"Let's lay it all out on the table."
This can mean "What's the scoop?" or "Let's have the facts"—but it can sometimes lead into ". . . tailor it to your situation."

"There's a right way to do things."
- *Forget the quick solution, I want you to run the whole obstacle course.*

This is an expensive notion; people seeking perfection should become artists, so their compulsions won't bother anyone else. Happily, lawyers tend to use it during the first office interview, and you can hire someone less persnickety.

"These things take time."
- *I don't know when it will get done.*
- *This cow is going to get milked till it's dry.*
- *Better jobs may come along and I'll have to put yours on the back burner.*
- *The bureaucracy is going to slow us down.*

The immediate response to this phrase is "How much time?"

"That's a gray area."
- If the lawyer continues ". . . but the way things have been recently, your odds of coming out OK are ____%," then it means exactly what he said.
- If he just stops, it means:
  - *I don't know.*
  - *No one knows; there's no clear law on that, and there haven't been enough cases to tell which way a court would swing.*
  - *I know but I'm too cautious to quote the odds (and get sued for malpractice) unless the customer seems realistic and insistent.*
  - *I know but I want to do some research.*

  Customers have been known to ask: "Does that mean my guess is as good as yours?" But don't dump a lawyer just for this phrase; ninety percent of them use it.

". . . an excess of zeal." Lawyer-to-lawyer insult.
- *You're rocking the boat.*
- *You're no gentleman.*

". . . acting in bad faith." A deadly lawyer-to-lawyer insult (bordering on the unforgivable "You're unethical.") It can mean:
- *You're rocking the boat.*
- *You're no gentleman.*
- *You're a liar.*

LAWYER'S LOGIC

"Those quick wits which . . . usurp the name of intelligence."
                                         Giuseppe di Lampedusa

Lawyer's logic can be strange brew—like philosophy that makes wonderful sense while you listen, and gets murky an hour later. Clear reasoning, unhappily, isn't the same as correct reasoning.

You can try to untangle bad logic. That takes time. You have to decide why it's bad before you can advance. It's often better to just ignore the lawyer's reasoning and go back to the beginning.

An acquaintance who works in a large law firm told me of the opening lecture she received on entering law school. A faculty member told the new students: "As you enter law school, your minds are like kaleidoscopes. When you leave here, your minds will be like laser beams." To which the lady added, "I was terrified!" I asked her what the other new students had thought. "They seemed to think it was a pretty good idea," she said. Ten years after the incident, there was still a faint look of horror on her face.

LEGAL PROBLEM—IS IT OR ISN'T IT?

If you're in jail, you have a legal problem. If jail weighs heavy on your mind, you have a legal problem. Otherwise—slow up!

Facts of Life:

1. Most businesses are happy to sell you something you don't need—and assure you it will solve life's problems. Cars improve your social life, vacations guarantee happiness, and so on.

2. Most businesses are happy to imply that failure and misery will come to those who don't buy the product.

3. Most businesses also discriminate between customers: people who have the money are sold hard, the others are ushered out.

4. If you can afford the product, most lawyers will sell you the product. Including honest ones, because:

> To a man with a hammer, everything looks like a nail.

You may need a lawyer to tell you what the law is—but you can't let a lawyer tell you that law is the only way to solve the problem.

The lawyer may be able to sum up the problem concisely. That's nice; it doesn't prove that his methods are better than yours. It doesn't even prove there is a problem.

(Anyway, that concise summation may turn into "It's not that simple" after a couple of days.)

LETTERS FROM THE LAWYER'S DESK

Review letters before they go out. Do they say what you want to say?

Lawyers tend to write aggressive letters that agree with their tough-guy self-image. Then, after throwing down the gauntlet, they encourage the customer to sue—sometimes to generate litigation, far more often because they don't want other lawyers to think they're weak.

Belligerent letters have their place—they can get results (FIRST USE, YES, p.70). But many an aggressive letter has been mailed that stunned the customer as much as the recipient; many a letter has made a neutral into an enemy.

The recipient may ignore a typical closing like "Thank you for your anticipated cooperation" as routine bad manners . . . but bad manners shouldn't be routine.

LETTERS OF INFORMATION

When you're not sure the lawyer jotted the right thing on the legal pad; when you didn't express the idea clearly; when there are some fine details—drop the lawyer a letter.

This is not a question of trust. The point is accurate communication.

LETTERS OF UNDERSTANDING
(aka LETTERS OF CONFIRMATION)

Are letters that start with:

". . . writing to make sure I understand . . ."

". . . writing to confirm our agreement . . ."

The letter then reiterates the points of your conversations, and finishes with ". . . please call if there is any misunderstanding."

These letters have four functions:

1. To make sure there is no misunderstanding.

2. To keep your lawyer's nose to the grindstone. People pay attention to letters.

3. To document the conversations.

4. To let the lawyer know you're a sophisticated customer who deserves better service than the other poor slobs.

Write the letter in a matter-of-fact way, without belligerence, suspicion, legal terminology, or certified mail receipts plastered to the envelope.

If any explanation seems necessary, tell the lawyer that you think more clearly on paper. That might not be the whole truth, but it ought to be the truth.

NOTES

When the money or stakes look serious, keep as many notes as you can stomach: conversations, facts, promises, money, times, dates, and places. Keep a telephone log.

When you meet your lawyer, take a pad and make notes. Aside from getting information, this will suggest you intend to monitor his performance—and a lawyer will subconsciously notice you're accumulating evidence as well as facts. (If you're obnoxious, he'll consciously notice.)

PHONE CALLS

The billing computer is probably turned on, so keep the call brisk. Write down the questions beforehand. But don't let the lawyer rush you; get your questions answered. Consultation is cheaper than getting the wrong job done.

See HYSTERIA *(p.13)*.

PHONE CALLS, UNRETURNED

A superb early warning sign.

Drop him. Before you need him. If you need him now, find a backup fast. Beware of FAST STARTS (p.66) with the backup.

(And if you absolutely can't drop him now, find a backup anyway. A few more weeks of frustration, and you may decide that you can afford to drop him, after all.)

Though lawyers can be incredibly slow in returning calls, you should expect some sort of contact from their office by the end of the next day, maximum. If it's urgent, a lot sooner than that. Despite their odd habits, this is still business, and a businessman who doesn't have time to return phone calls must have more work than he can handle. Take your job to someone with free time. You'll have plenty of company. Unreturned calls rank near the top as a cause for dismissal.

The majority of lawyers will take calls immediately from a prospective customer. This tells you nothing about the future. The lawyer may continue to be accessible, or he may start ignoring your calls once you're part of the client list.

PROCEEDING, AGAINST YOUR LAWYER'S ADVICE

Law—like life in general—contains endless possible troubles. In life we learn that some of the possibilities just aren't all that important.

Likewise, legal considerations aren't always that important. Sometimes a problem seems less serious after you've asked a few questions, so you decide to ignore the lawyer's advice, or take only part of it. Meanwhile, he's giving you cautionary glances, mumbling "gray areas" and "it's not that simple . . ."

But it is that simple. You'll never know everything there is to know about the situation. As in the rest of life, sooner or later, you have to take your best shot.

When? It depends—but there is one theory I keep coming back to:

Line up your ducks. When the big ducks are in line . . . shoot.

PROJECT MANAGEMENT

There are **tasks**, like writing a simple will. A task isn't defined by the fact that there's only one product. It's because once you and the lawyer finish talking, there's only one thing that needs doing—sit down and write the will.

From the customer's point of view, it's a task if you understand what you're getting, when you'll get it, and what it will cost. You keep notes and a file, of course—but you feel comfortable with a rough plan of action.

A **project** contains many tasks. It might be a lawsuit. It could also be a will—for Howard Hughes. You know what you want, perhaps—but you're not sure if that's what you're getting. As to when and how much, you're lost.

If that describes what you're getting into, you need a project mentality. You're the general contractor. The lawyer is the sub-contractor. You want the big three of any project:

The Right Results, On Time, Within Budget

The lawyer may tell you the job is routine. Fine. But if the complexity makes you uncomfortable, it's a project.

THE PROJECT PLAN

Defining the Question

See INTERVIEWING (p.101).

Defining the Project   *This is the point where you need new methods.*

- Ask for a description of the steps to completing the job. Make a timetable as you listen. This may look like alphabet soup on a string—a list of motions, filings, writs, etc, with dates scrawled after them. At the end, though, there should be a word that makes sense: "Finished!"

- Go back to the beginning, and ask the lawyer, "What is the worst that is likely to happen?" Get a rough timetable and cost for the worst scenarios. You may have to be persistent.

Go or No-Go: *Does the boss (you) approve this solution?*

- Tell the lawyer you'll get back to him, leave, and think it out:
  - Do the steps make sense—as you read the consumer legal dictionary that you bought this afternoon?
  - Does the timetable add up?
  - Does the money add up?
  - Is this going to get satisfactory results?
  - Is a legal solution best?

  If you call back with a "go," then "agree" on the goal of the project. Before hanging up, you want to hear the lawyer say the same thing you're saying, in words you can understand.

Production: *Making it happen—now the timetable is boss.*

- Get a soft pencil, a big eraser, a ruler, and a big piece of paper.

- At the far right side of the paper, write "Finished!" Then start filling in the big three:

Time
- Starting from the left, write down the things that need to happen to reach the finish. Make a box for each "milestone." Write the date it's supposed to happen above the box. When the task is done, check off the milestone box and write the date. Watch the dates.

Money
- Write the total quote under "Finished!"

- As you cross each milestone, add the running total to the timetable.

Ideally the running total is coming off the monthly bills. If there are no monthly bills, estimate the billable hours from your own notes. And ask a few questions, like "What's the current bill? *Are the costs on track?*" You may have to persist a bit; lawyers tend to answer money questions with "I don't know, the billing office handles that."

Look ahead—when you get to "Finished!," will the billable hours add up to the quote? Or is the bill getting ahead of the work done? If the bill's getting too far ahead, it's time to give the lawyer a call and ask why.

Results

- Along the bottom of the sheet, write your comments on how things are going—whether you're on track for the right results. These are your opinions, not the lawyer's. Basically, the comments should tell you that you're happy.

Finish

- Keep going until you cross the finish line.

Notes

By the time the project is over, the chart will be a mess. Very few project plans survive contact with reality. But project charts do have a way of getting you to the results.

Figure on spending an hour or two a month on this. This is probably about the same amount of time you'll spend worrying if you let the lawyer handle everything.

Managing the project is also a form of managing the lawyer.

The most reliable results come when you follow the timeline like a hunter on the trail.

Let the lawyer know you have a calendar. Don't let him know you have a timeline laid out, or he may just leave scheduling to you.

WHAT LAWYERS WILL DO LEFT TO THEMSELVES

If you never call for a progress report, a lawyer will do one of several things:

- Nothing.

- Research.

- Consult with other lawyers.

- Do as much of the job as he can and wait for you to call.

- Do as much of the job as he can and then call you.

- Finish the job.

This seems like a vague list, but consider: if you take your car to the auto repair shop, you may have some worries. Do those worries include the shop:

- Doing nothing?

- Reading about your car (and charging for it)?

- Calling other mechanics to discuss it (and charging for it)?

- Doing half the job and then pushing the car out in the parking lot to wait for your call?

No. You know that the shop will head toward completing the job. Your concerns are whether they'll do it right, and whether the price will be fair.

Lawyers have more ways to go astray.

Keep in touch.

YOU MIGHT BE THE EXPERT

Some days you reach a point where you have to conclude that you know more than the lawyers.

Nuts and Bolts Expert

Many business people know legal nuts and bolts extremely well. I've never been in the position myself, but I've known business people who—within their field—knew how to write a contract and if necessary file a suit and walk it through court and collect a judgment better than most lawyers in that town (including most of the specialists).

This shouldn't amaze you; people with persistent illnesses often become experts on their own problem, eventually learning more about it than the average doctor does.

Legal Explorer

Is a more worrisome position to find yourself. When even a specialist's opinion doesn't make sense in light of the recent legislation you read about; when you get the feeling the specialist hasn't heard of that recent legislation; when you're considering calling some law professor on the other side of the country, who wrote a book on the subject—you're close to becoming the only expert in town. (I once had a lawyer ask—dubiously—where I had heard of some recent legislation. So I told him the truth: "Last week, in Time magazine." It's funny now, but it made me nervous at the time.)

If this "instant expert" status makes you nervous, it should. At *best* this means—as far as this area of law is concerned—that you'll be flying solo from now on. No quick phone calls to clear up a question. At worst, you could end up with a court case, and no lawyer capable of handling it—until you've paid him to spend 50 hours in the library, studying up on the subject.

Don't dispense with lawyers when you find you're the expert. You still may need one to handle the details. You want him to go over your plan—using your working assumptions—and make sure it's otherwise solid. This may be painful for the lawyer, but he's probably been through it once or twice before.

YOU'RE ON YOUR OWN, PAL

When the lawyer can't get past "that's a gray area." Persistent, you ask further questions like, "OK, let's look at the worst scenario. Let's say I end up in court. How many cases like this have been won or lost in the last year?"

"Hrmph, well, each case is different . . ."

"Well, have there been any cases at all like this in the last few years? How thick is the case law?" (i.e. "How many pages' worth of cases are there in the law books?")

By now the conversation is sliding over the edge of a bottomless pit. Sometimes the lawyer just doesn't want the job. More often, either it is a gray area, and your guess is as good as theirs—or you need a more knowledgeable lawyer.

This situation frequently leads to <u>YOU</u> MIGHT BE THE EXPERT (p.89).

Finding and Hiring

"To be lucky in the beginning is everything."   Cervantes

And when it came to lawyers, I was very lucky. Which accounts for my attitude towards legal services; the first lawyers I did business with were good lawyers and good human beings. Nowadays I don't like to settle for less.

You may not be so lucky. But you are more thorough than I am; you have bought this book. You intend to make a plan. That's why the book was written; read it, and you can travel a second road to luck:

"Chance favors the prepared mind."   Louis Pasteur

Finding the right lawyer stops half your legal problems before they start. Because it can be done, it's worth shopping. Because it's not easy, you should squarely face . . .

THE ODDS OF FINDING
A GOOD LAWYER

These numbers are my own rough estimate. They may be wrong for your time and place—but if you don't have much experience with lawyers, a rough estimate is better than none.

The Basic Wish List, and the chances of filling it.

Intelligent	60%
Accessible	40%
Understandable	40%
Effective	35%
Understands customer goals	30%
Writes reasonable bills	25%
Doesn't need to be more important than the customer	20%
Deals with customers as individuals	20%

Nice Extras

Imaginative legal solutions	10%
Imaginative non-legal solutions	1%
Common-sense solutions	2%

This doesn't seem that bad until you try to find all these characteristics in one lawyer.

On the dark side, at least 20% of lawyers are completely beyond redemption. It adds up to this: you have to work. Now on to finding the right one . . .

MAKING THE FIRST CUT:
Do You Need a Specialist?

There are a few jobs that most competent lawyers can handle, and jobs that only half a dozen lawyers in the country can handle.

The second situation isn't all bad. You need just one lawyer. It's easier to choose from a group of six than a group of thousands. Sometimes easier to find a good one, too, because extreme specialization will narrow down the field fast; once you get the first couple of leads, the same names keep turning up—and the same recommendations.

The list below categorizes regular, garden-variety jobs. A will involving 17 cousins or $4 million calls for greater specialization; so does a divorce that involves another country's laws.

Jobs That Most Lawyers Can Handle

Simple wills.

Slightly Specialized Work

Family Law, including divorce; Personal Injury; Drunk Driving; Residential Real Estate; Tenant.

Specialized Work

Business/Incorporation; Corporate (bigger business); Commercial Real Estate; Landlord; Criminal; Tax; Immigration; Labor; Worker's Compensation; and most anything dealing with state regulation.

Very Specialized

Admiralty; International; Copyright; Trademarks; Patents; Entertainment; Environmental; and most Federal regulation.

Fair Warning: When lawyers have a legal question, they look for a lawyer who deals with that job regularly. If you want exceptional results, start thinking in the same direction. My own view is somewhat broader—I want someone who knows how, but it doesn't have to be a lawyer. A knowledgeable business associate or paralegal will do.

MAKING THE SECOND CUT

Needs vary. That's why I've included the sections on TYPES OF LEGAL BUSINESSES and TYPES OF LAWYERS. However, if you want a quick opinion, this is my own working attitude:

There isn't always a second cut. Since there aren't that many lawyers who are all-around good, I take them where I can find them—and if they're working in a big firm, I just try to ignore the overpriced office space, the overpriced furniture, the pomp, and the circumstances.

Given a choice, though, I steer towards sole practitioners or two- to three-person firms. They're usually cheaper in the short run, almost always in the long run, and they're not so agitated. If I'm hiring within a firm, I aim for junior partners or senior associates. Again, this is when I have a choice.

When I go looking, I try connections first. If none of them are handy, I try the techniques on p.97-99.

If I don't even know where to start, I ask connections, or call a telephone lawyer and ask what kind of specialist I need.

My needs don't run to million-dollar lawsuits, so I don't need battalions of lawyers. In the small businesses I've run, I don't mind dealing with four separate lawyers. In fact, I prefer it; it keeps me from getting complacent. If I turned all my jobs over to one big firm, I might develop the delusion that the firm was looking at the big picture, and applying the art of foresight to my business.

HOT LEADS

The best way to find a good lawyer is through a recommendation from someone:

- Who has good judgment.

- Who really knows how the lawyer works.

Recommendation is a method I constantly see in print, but examine reality for a moment. How many of your acquaintances have good judgment? How many know how the lawyer works? And how many of your friends know a lawyer who has experience in your type of problem?

People Who Might Know the Right Specialist

When canvassing personal connections, ask yourself which group of acquaintances might have hired that type of lawyer. Some obvious sources: immigration—immigrants; copyright—writers; business—businessmen; incorporation—someone who started their own corporation. (If these people don't know outright, they should be close to the people who do know.)

People Who Know a Lot of Lawyers

Five groups who hire lawyers frequently:

- Troublemakers and chiselers.

- People born without a lick of sense.

- Business owners.

- Rich people.

- The truly unfortunate.

STARTING COLD

If there are no realistic hot leads, move on to the basic rule: shop <u>hard</u>.

The Sampling Theory

There are plenty of lawyers out there. You probably need just one. The normal method is to take the first lawyer who comes along, and try to live with him. More persistent customers sometimes sample two or three and pick the most promising one.

There is a system that finds a better lawyer in less time, with less stress:

Starting from the whole pool of possibles, make a list of anywhere from three to thirty names. The more credible your sources are, the fewer names you need: if you're getting recommendations from three law school professors, and they all understand what you're looking for, three should be plenty.

If you're going through the Yellow Pages, list thirty names. Do it fast. Cut names off the list for anything you don't like. (If you're starting off this way—ice cold—plan to spend two hours on the phone before you find even one possibility. The first hour will give you the feel of the territory; the second hour you start zeroing in.)

Read INTERVIEWING (p. 101) and start calling. When you have a list of three who seem like they can handle the job, visit the one you feel you can get along with best. If the interview shows you can't get along, try the others on your final list of three.

This seems like a lot of work. Maybe. But it usually takes much less time than interviewing two or three lawyers who don't give you confidence, and then sweating over the choice.

If it's a small job, this seems like too much work. Maybe. And maybe that small job will grow by a few hundred dollars and a few months if you hire the wrong lawyer.

PLACES TO START

Business and professional associations may have a good list. The person who answers the association's phone will know nothing. A couple of levels up, they should know. Don't make them clam up by asking for recommendations. Just ask, "Who do the members seem to be satisfied with?"

If that person won't tell, the association newsletter may. (I wouldn't go to that much trouble unless it was an important job.)

People who are in the same line of work . . . but don't handle that type of job. This is a good system in any industry. The best auto mechanic in town probably knows which shop does the best auto body repair. The owner of that Mexican restaurant on the corner won't tell you which Mexican restaurants are best—they're his competitors— but the owner of that great Italian restaurant may have an opinion. The company that did a fine job installing your air-conditioning should know the good electricians. Some of these people may think you're strange; others will understand the logic.

Applying the theory to law, imagine that you have a real estate question. You also have the names of three well-respected real estate lawyers, and one tax lawyer recommended as "whip-smart, and a really nice guy."

Throw the three well-respected lawyers in the trash can. Call the tax lawyer. Don't ask him for a "referral." Make him think; ask, "Who would *you* see if you had a job like this?"

A solid recommendation usually comes with a dash of enthusiasm— without any feeling of hard sell.

Law school registrars. They've seen the kids become lawyers. They have a sense of what makes them tick. Some of the students are working in the area. Reports trickle back.

The registrar also knows which professors practice on the side. The professors are almost always high in expertise; they are probably good candidates for jobs where you want the latest scoop on broad issues (including what the higher courts are ruling this week). They are rarely greedy. On the downside, they may be distinctly indecisive (being academics), as well as being less familiar with standard local methods and courthouse rigmarole.

Registrars vary; this doesn't always work. In any case don't tell the registrar I sent you.

Law school professors . On second thought, call a professor first. If he doesn't have a recommendation, he may fill you in on the registrar.

Keep in mind that all these people are doing you a favor. They're not earning money talking to you, and they don't want to take the blame (or get sued) if things go wrong. So tread lightly. Don't ask for a guarantee, and don't pump them for free legal advice.

GENERIC METHODS

The local or state **bar association referral service** should give you a list of people who handle your type of job. (They don't make recommendations, and if they did, there would be no reason to take them seriously.)

If the job is writing a will, their list is useless; a phone book could do as much. If the job is something obscure—like admiralty law—their list can save you hours of phone calls. In between, it's worth a try.

HALT (in Washington, DC) is a consumer organization aimed at legal reform. They have a modest list of recommended lawyers around the country. HALT members are relatively sophisticated customers, so the list should be reliable.

The **National Lawyer's Guild**, found in most major metropolitan telephone books. This is an association of lawyers who describe themselves as progressive. Many of the members are former radicals who have grown up but not sold out. Idealistic, but not necessarily bleeding at the heart. My understanding is that they don't force their politics on their own customers (of course that doesn't mean they'll buy <u>your</u> politics).

Some chapters do referrals, others don't; some chapters even have a recording saying they don't.

Lists of which lawyers have been winning their cases. There's some merit to this theory. A drawback, too, since these are also lists of which lawyers solve their customers' problems by going to court.

The Yellow Pages. Some specialties do a lot of advertising. Of course, most of the splashy advertisers look like shysters, but there are some that give facts without hoopla. In some phone books lawyers are also listed by specialty (though the specialty listings are rarely complete).

METHODS TO SKIP

Legal referral services that charge the lawyers for a listing. Would you listen to a restaurant critic who was taking money from the restaurants?

DOUBLE CHECKING YOUR SELECTION

Directories of lawyers (the Martindale-Hubbell is the best known) are found at many public libraries.

These vary from a couple of thousand listings to over half a million (the M-H). The directories typically give brief biographies, a mention of specialization, and sometimes ratings. Some have indexes by specialization, some don't. Since the biographies are often written by the lawyers themselves, and the ratings given by their fellow lawyers, these directories tell somewhat more about their public relations and political talent than their legal ability. Still, it's an indication.

A WARNING ON CONTINGENCY CASES

Be especially careful in choosing the right lawyer. Once you sign a contingency contract, you can still fire him, but you may have trouble hiring another—because with the usual contingency contract, the first lawyer still gets a percentage of the fee.

See CONTRACTS *(p.120).*

INTERVIEWING

Know-how is the first target. It lies close to a firm quote, and leads onward to results.

Drive, brains, and honesty may produce the same result at the same price—but how long will it take to find all three in one lawyer? Always try to make know-how the first target.

What To Do

Write down what you want—and what you'll be satisfied with.

Scan the starter questions, and the interview charts on p.104-105. Write down the questions.

Make the telephone call. Run through the starter questions, and a couple of extras if needed. Make notes. Then go back to the interview charts and compare.

(Ignore hard sellers. Tell 'em you'll have to consider their words of wisdom.)

A Starter Set of Questions

Always ask these questions:

What's my legal situation?
Should generate some kind of response.

What are the legal options?
It will probably take an office visit to get this question answered. If you know exactly what you want done—tell him. See if he can work with customers who make their own game plans.

How many jobs like this have you yourself completed?
I think this is a rude question, but I ask anyway. There's too much billing-for-education going on in the legal trade.

What are the odds?

May take an office visit to get this answered. Some lawyers believe that quoting odds verges on unethical behavior. You need a lawyer who has gotten past this unrealistic notion.

You can't expect a lawyer to put the odds on paper, because too many naïve customers think that "80%" is the same as "100%." When things go wrong, they sue. But two rational adults should be able to agree that "the odds" doesn't mean "guaranteed."

How much? Or, more diplomatically: "How much will this cost?"

Don't make the question any longer than that. You already have a song-and-dance coming. A vague question will make the dance longer, if not endless.

When can it be done? How long will it take?

May generate another song-and-dance. For large jobs see PROJECT MANAGEMENT (p.85), on setting timetables.

Consider these if the conversation keeps rolling:

Are there any decent non-legal options out there?

This is a hard question to phrase. You're just trying to see if he's seen any of his customers come up with ingenious solutions—but it may be interpreted as an invitation to personal advice. And if you say ". . . good non-legal options," the lawyer's caution will take over, and he'll say "No."

How many jobs do you typically handle at the same time?

Which leads on, of course, to "how many are you handling now?" If you have a big job coming up, you need to know this. This is the most discreet way I know to ask what is fundamentally an impolite question, since it implies the lawyer can't manage his time . . . which is exactly your concern. A lawyer probably shouldn't be handling more than fifty active jobs—though there might be another hundred sitting on the back burner, waiting for decisions from bureaucrats, court dates, etc.

Are you licensed to practice in this state?

I don't think I'd bother to ask in the middle of Texas. In an area where different jurisdictions border—like New York City, or Washington, DC—the question should be asked. Frequently a partner will take on a job and then have an associate sign all the papers. This may be OK—but you ought to know in advance.

Are you licensed in this specialized court (e.g. tax court, Supreme Court, . . .)?

Unnecessary question for most customers—of the jobs bound for court, most go to municipal or circuit court.

The big question that will be answered for you:

Does the lawyer want cash up front? How much? A deposit, just to make sure you're serious? Full payment in advance? Or somewhere in between?

A demand for full payment in advance should make you consider another lawyer, because cash up front has a way of evaporating, even if the job turns out to be simple. It can evaporate even faster if you fire the lawyer.

First Interview—Telephone

Someone who doesn't know how to do the job (but is willing to give it a try)	*Someone who knows how to do the job*
• never offers a complete solution on the phone	• rarely offers a complete solution on the phone
• wants you to spell out the problem	• gets the drift
• laboriously analyzes the situation when you ask if he's done the job before	• says, "That's a regular part of my business," or "That's all I do."
• talks about the breadth of his firm's experience	• says he can do it
• tries to impress	• why try to impress, when the job's no big deal?
• wants to tailor the job to your needs (this is sometimes a warning sign of greed rather than missing know-how)	• there are a couple of points to decide on, but the job is fairly routine
• is tense	• is matter-of-fact; if tense, it's not because of your job

Second Interview—In Person

Someone who doesn't know how to do the job	*Someone who knows how to do the job*
• wants to know more about the problem	• wants to know what you want done
• makes notes on everything	• makes notes on the unique aspects of your situation, and what you want done
• needs the papers before he can do anything	• "I'll need to take a look at them" (but it's not the first issue)
• will call you	• lays out some of the legal situation
• can't give a quote	• can give a ballpark figure for routine jobs, and a range for truly unique jobs
• talks about hourly rate, can't be more specific	• may tell you the hourly rate, but gets on toward the total without a wrestling match
• talks around the job, or says it's a "challenge"	• is matter-of-fact; may be mildly interested by your story, but not especially challenged; sometimes so un-talkative you begin to worry if he knows anything at all

Other Points

- Don't make the lawyer feel he's one of fifty names on a checklist. *Do* make him aware that he's dealing with an equation: cost vs. results. If he meets the equation, he gets the work. If not, no work. Impressing or intimidating the customer won't change the decision process. This attitude won't particularly bother a lawyer who has the right product at the right price.

- Looking for bonuses:

  —Can you get along with this lawyer?

  —Can you rely on him? If he were a horse, would you buy him?

- Personal favorites . . . I like to:

  —hear lawyers voluntarily talk about how they bill (the specifics—almost anyone will tell you his hourly rate these days).

  —hear them tell me that paralegals and clerks will be doing some of the work.

  —hear that some of the tasks are quick work.

  —be told what work I can do myself, or have done more cheaply elsewhere.

- Over years of phone interviews I've come to see shopping for lawyers the same way I see shopping for window cleaning or driveway resurfacing. I get on the phone and start calling. Either they sell that service, they don't sell it, or they have something they claim is better. If they're in the ballpark, and I like the feel of them, I'll go take a look. Sometimes I change my mind and buy the "better" service. Usually the company is too far off base, and I keep on dialing until I find someone who has the right service.

Types of Legal Businesses

MEDIUM TO BIG FIRMS

Pros

- Impress people (e.g. bankers and other bureaucrats).

- More likely to be able to handle all your jobs.

- More flexible in handling huge, sudden workloads (though how well they are handled will vary).

I mention these last two with hesitation, because very few firms, small or large, can respond with the speed of a first-class sole practitioner. By the time a firm gets out of the gate, the sole practitioner might be through the learning curve and headed down the back straightaway.

Cons

- High priced.

- Conflicts of interest are more likely as the firm gets bigger. The most obvious instance is also the least likely: one of your competitors or adversaries is a customer of another lawyer in the firm. The salesman may pontificate about ethics and Chinese walls (no discussion allowed between lawyers) . . . Consider another firm.

Or a competitor is a former customer of the firm. Former? What defines former? Consider another firm.

A spiritual conflict of interest is more common. You're being sued for allowing a burglar to break his leg on your property, and the firm you're considering does the bulk of its work in personal injury. You say: "Well, they sure know how the opposition works." True. But can you rely on them to fight hammer-and-tongs against the very type of customer who provides their bread and butter? Maybe. Maybe not.

Walking in the Door

Usually you call a firm asking for one specific lawyer who was recommended; you talk to the lawyer, check his know-how, discuss the specifics of billing, and decide whether to hire the lawyer, whereupon the firm comes along as part of the deal.

(Even if you do ask for a particular lawyer, the firm may try to sell you another one. You may have to insist.)

However, sometimes you end up at a certain firm out of exhaustion or desperation: you figure from their reputation or size that they must have someone who can do the job. If you don't have a lawyer in mind, that becomes the first issue.

A cold call will be passed to a senior partner (the partner is usually a working lawyer, taking his turn at sales, but he may be purely a salesman). If you let him take charge, he'll assign you a lawyer based on the firm's own criteria.

The first part of the firm's criteria is whether you're operating as an individual or a business—that is, are you a free range chicken, who lays an egg occasionally, or a dairy cow, who can be milked regularly?

If you're a chicken, the next step is to feel you out and determine the size of your bank account—that is, just how big a chicken you are. Tiny chickens go to junior associates, small to medium go to senior associates, medium to large go to partners. If you were referred by one of their big chicken or milk cow customers, this may move you up the scale (not necessarily what you want).

If you're the average chicken, this means you start off talking to a partner (the salesman)—and then get kicked downstairs.

This is not necessarily bad. You should be paying less. And while the salesman may assign you a junior associate, you will probably be offered a junior partner or senior associate. Without a specific lawyer in mind, that's where you want to be anyway.

See LEVELS OF EXPERIENCE *, p.116.*

Curiously, the size of the egg you're about to lay doesn't seem to count all that much. How often you lay eggs is even less important.

If you're a milk cow, you go to a partner, probably senior. (Rich, inexperienced individuals are also herded in with the milk cows.)

Note

Big firms tend to be hired for big jobs. If your job is big, there will be several lawyers working on it. Always have a brief conference with *all* the lawyers working on your job to make sure:

- They know a human being is their customer (this transfers some of their loyalty to the customer, where it belongs).

- They know <u>what the goal is</u>.

- You know who's supposedly working on your job.

SMALL FIRMS

Small firms don't have a variety of experience levels; there are partners and a few associates.

The small firm can be ideal. There is more knowledge on call than most sole practitioners have in their head. Yet overhead is still controllable. The pressure to overbill is theoretically reduced. At its best the small firm combines the best features of the sole practitioner and the larger firm.

It often works out, but not always. In the small firm it's theoretically possible for everyone to stay abreast of each other's work much better than in a large firm; if your lawyer is away, another can pinch-hit. Fine. The problem arises when the others don't stay abreast; they keep pinch-hitting anyway. Which gives you two or three lawyers to coordinate, and none of them in charge of your job. In a big firm there's always someone *pretending* to be in charge of your job; at least you know who to yell at.

SOLE PRACTITIONERS

For the average person, this can be best. At least it's familiar. Even in a climate of increasing specialization, there are sole practitioners willing to be the equivalent of a family doctor. The most common jobs and questions (particularly questions) can be handled at a reasonable cost, and—one hopes—the lawyer will come to know you and your legal requirements through a gradual series of preventative jobs.

Though a sole practitioner may say his rate is $150 an hour, you can be fairly sure the final bill will be smaller than the bill from a $150-an-hour big firm; usually a lot smaller. There are two cautions.

First, he had better be good; there's no one to catch his mistakes. Second, he needs enough confidence to refer you to someone else when the job is outside his expertise. Which could be often, no matter how good he is.

For small-business customers, the sole practitioner can also be best, for the same reasons the average person might have. The difference is that even a very small business may need help in more than one area of law, so may need more than one sole practitioner. The businessman will then have to coordinate the overall legal plan. Is that a nuisance? Maybe; it takes time. But it's also incentive to learn a bit about law and different specialties, and in my mind a businessman *must* know a bit— at least enough to judge what services he needs.

For big-business customers, sole practitioners rarely serve. The work is usually too broad for one lawyer's knowledge, and the sudden workload usually more than the sole practitioner can handle. In theory the big business could hire top-notch sole practitioners and coordinate the plan themselves. In practice this is unlikely, due to big business's love affair with consultants and experts, which leads them to put their whole legal future in the hands of the lawyers.

LEGAL SERVICE PLANS

These are sometimes sold through a storefront legal office, but more commonly an organizer contracts a variety of lawyers to provide services under a set fee plan, which then comes to the customer via junk mail. The offer is something like: "Sign up now for $50, and when you call one of our broad team of experts will be ready to serve you at a discount from their regular rate," or "You will be referred to an attorney in your own area who is a member of the plan."

I've never used these services; they may a good buy for an individual who has a regular need for quick advice. Three potential problems are visible.

First: Is the advice any good at all? Is there any effort to provide specialized advice? Or is it grab-bag hiring?

Second: beyond a few hours of service, many of these contracts put you back to regular fees.

Third: Unless it was a phone conversation, how does the customer know that the lawyer didn't actually charge his regular rate—by falsifying the hours?

In both the second and third issues, there's a potential for bait-and-switch sales tactics. Generally, these plans look suspect; who wants to pay both a lawyer and an organizer?

Possible Exceptions

A few of these plans offer some interesting services:

- Unlimited telephone consultations (brief, I suppose).

- Review of short documents (real estate contracts, etc.).

- Letters written "on your behalf."
  (I assume they're offering "threatening letter service." But are the letters on engraved stationery, or mass-produced on a cheap printer? Deadbeats and businesses will instantly recognize cheap letters as idle threats.)

STOREFRONT LAW OFFICES

In general, inexperienced lawyers and high turnover. Once beyond the chop suey menu, the fees are not much lower than those of a decent sole practitioner.

The walk-in accessibility is noteworthy, and this style of law may have a future, but for now I would think of them as a convenient paper mill, a place to get very simple wills or uncontested divorces. (The store should have a prominent list of standard prices.)

TELEPHONE LAWYERS

A recent development found in California. It will probably spread. There isn't any category established in the Yellow Pages; you have to search through the "Attorneys" listings.

They charge by the minute for telephone consultation or review of documents. The pure telephone lawyers don't take on complete jobs, so the potential for overbilling is limited. This is a decent system for customers who know what the facts are and what they need. The information in hand, they can either act on it themselves, move on to a regular lawyer, or skip it completely.

It doesn't work quite so well for customers who know nothing about the law. Though there isn't any great profit at stake, telephone lawyers may still try to answer when they just don't have enough knowledge. I suggest that customers who know nothing ask: "If this is outside your area of expertise, could you lay out some of the situation for me, and tell me what kind of specialist I need?" That way the lawyer gets to accomplish something, and the customer gets himself past the stage of complete ignorance for twenty or thirty dollars.

Some of these services also send copies of pertinent laws and magazine articles, either cheap or free. They usually understand that I want a law magazine article containing a quick opinion, not five hundred pages of case law (descriptions of specific cases).

A telephone lawyer is not the perfect lawyer, but the low-stress style of work does seem to reduce attitude problems, and even the most timid customer can cut off a conversation in a few minutes.

PARALEGALS

Independent paralegals are setting up shop in increasing numbers, offering services such as adoptions, uncontested divorces, simple contracts, powers of attorney, simple wills, incorporation, and probate. These jobs fall into two categories: jobs that don't involve the courtroom at all, and jobs that involve standing in front of the judge and answering a few yes-or-no questions.

A lot of these jobs are no big deal once you know how. Before you know how, they're a pain, because there's just no apparatus to inform the citizens. Court clerks will help you if you know how to deal with them— but one wrong question, revealing you're a rookie, and they'll say, "We can't give legal advice." Lacking legal know-how, you don't even know *if* you can do it.

So do the paralegals perform these jobs as well as lawyers? Probably. The paralegals may not understand the ramifications as well as the lawyers—but lawyers rarely give their full attention to simple jobs. They use boilerplate contracts and standardized solutions, usually created by more specialized lawyers.

Is a paralegal more likely than a lawyer to botch a job outright? Maybe less. Paralegals are under fire from the lawyers' guild for the "unauthorized practice of law," and they don't have a bar association to protect them from outraged customers; they have good reason to be cautious. On the average I have fair confidence in paralegals for jobs that involve *doing something*. In jobs such as "what if" research, I'm less confident that they understand what I'm after. That is, they're better on what *does happen* than what *might happen*. Warning: "Legal typing schools" are proliferating, producing instant paralegals. This is not the same education a paralegal gets by doing research and form-filling in the trenches, at a lawyer's office.

What can't paralegals handle? Jobs where they are excluded by the legal or social rules. A paralegal can't represent you in court, because it's illegal. He probably can't represent you at a multi-million dollar transaction, because he doesn't have "expert power." So in theory hiring a paralegal can leave you dead-ended. But as long as you realize that in time, it's going to be a comparatively inexpensive dead end.

Levels of Experience (Within the Firms)

THE TOTEM POLE

In a firm large enough to offer different grades, you can divide the lawyers into: senior partners, junior partners, senior associates, and junior associates. The firms themselves may have finer gradations, but those have more to do with pecking order than experience.

The informal grading system is: finders, minders, and grinders. Finders are senior partners who supervise, act as salesmen, handle jobs that demand big-league networking, and review documents produced by minders. Minders are junior partners and senior associates who deal with the customers and produce the bulk of the final work. Grinders are junior associates who do research and draft papers.

Then there are the non-persons: legal secretaries and paralegals. Legal secretaries, while they are often unusually capable, generally stick close to secretarial work. Paralegals are another matter; they do a lot of the grinding. Unless you are very close to a lawyer, you will never, never deal with a paralegal from start to finish of a job. Part of the job will always be funneled through the lawyer's hands, whether he's needed or not. But there are two reasons to keep paralegals in mind. First, some of them do legal work independently, as described in (p.115). Second, lawyers have a tendency to bill paralegal work on attorney timesheets. This is almost impossible to prove in any one instance—but you can look for patterns.

JUNIOR PARTNERS AND SENIOR ASSOCIATES

There isn't much difference in experience between a junior partner and a senior associate; they've both put in enough time to have learned, assuming they are going to learn. A junior partner typically has 8 to 15 years experience; a senior associate, 6 to 9 years. There's not that much difference in hourly rates.

I prefer either one to a junior associate, because they can get the job done faster with fewer mistakes.

I prefer them to senior partners because:

- The junior partners/senior associates have lower hourly rates.

- They're less likely to have someone down the totem pole do the work while billing it as their own.

- Sometimes they're better than senior partners—less experienced, but with equal know-how, and not so complacent.

About Senior Associates

- In boom times, the senior associates may be leaving soon (if they don't make partner). This could be a problem if your job drags on.

- Law firms often treat associates as interchangeable parts.

  When you find an associate you like, make sure the partners understand that you consider that associate your lawyer from then on; that if the firm wants to rely on your business, it has to assign that lawyer to your jobs. Otherwise, the firm may keep bouncing you back and forth between the associate and one (or more) of the other lawyers. (If a partner has time, then he'll put in as much time as possible, since he can bill more than the associate.)

Asking for a particular associate produces benefits beyond continuity:

- The associate feels that someone wants him. He's not just a faceless paper-producer for the high-billing partner.

- He gets the satisfaction of seeing a job through to the end.

SENIOR PARTNERS

Senior partners generally have more experience than the juniors. Sometimes that benefits you; sometimes it doesn't. Seniors don't always consider the details as carefully as they should. That can be an expensive way to cut your throat.

Six reasons it might make sense to hire a senior partner:

- A specific area of know-how.

- Political connections.

- Financial connections.

- Image. Seeing your lawyer's name right on the letterhead impresses people. It particularly impresses other lawyers.

- Wisdom (but antique furniture doesn't guarantee wisdom).

- Business judgment (but a corner office doesn't guarantee business judgment).

Your financial burdens should be smaller if you can hire a junior partner, and just bring in the senior when necessary.

JUNIOR ASSOCIATES

Don't expect law firms to screen inexperienced lawyers away from the customers. Everyone is supposed to produce billable hours. Many of the juniors produce their hours by doing research. This is all right. Research ability depends on daily practice as much as overall experience. However, when the need arises, the firm will outfit the juniors with nicer offices and a few customers.

This may give them responsibility, but it won't give them know-how; junior associates produce more than their share of bungled jobs. There's little benefit to the customer in running this risk—though they cost less per hour, they usually wipe out the savings by taking more hours. (Sometimes a partner will slice a few hours from the bill if it's taken too long. But don't count on it.)

If the juniors working on your job are hidden away, their ability theoretically doesn't matter, since a more experienced lawyer is supposed to be checking their work. (It's still a good idea to bring the juniors into a conference early in the game. See MEDIUM TO BIG FIRMS, p. 107.)

On the other hand, if a junior associate is "going to be handling your case," supervision drops off. Then it's up to you to discriminate: is he the careful, thinking type?

Or have you been assigned an overconfident puppy? Is he prematurely suffering from lawyer's disrespect? Is his wardrobe getting ahead of his career?

Youth in itself doesn't make a puppy. True puppies are brash and arrogant, or eager and gullible—and always more ignorant than they realize. If necessary, call the salesman for a change of lawyers.

(In deal making, lawyer-to-lawyer power dynamics have to be considered. If you send a junior associate somewhere to negotiate for you, and the other side sends a senior partner, will your lawyer be able to stand up to their lawyer?)

Big Details

CONTRACTS

A contract can be important, but it's the last step in hiring a lawyer. A contract won't guarantee competence, know-how, honesty, or results; you need to think about those details well before you start making contracts. Here are eight general ways to go about a contract. Starting from the least fine print:

1. No written contract at all. This is common.

Most customers who go this route are used to lawyers and law, or they have a solid relationship with the lawyer. No contract can still be risky. If you don't fit in those groups, having no contract moves towards recklessness.

2. A letter from the lawyer to the customer, stating what the hourly rate is and briefly mentioning the job. This is probably the most common form of contract.

This is a contract, but not a good one. Convert it to a #3 by sending a LETTER OF UNDERSTANDING (p.80) back to the lawyer, filling in the missing points. Keep notes and a phone log; this will confirm and re-confirm.

3. A letter from the lawyer to the customer, mentioning what the job is, when it will be done, and how much it's expected to cost.

The customer then nails down the commitment with a return letter outlining any other key points, such as:

- Any changes in billing methods or additional charges will be only by mutual agreement (in other words, no "value added" charges).

- How often bills are to be sent, and whether they will be broken down by task.

- That the lawyer will notify the customer promptly if it appears the final cost will exceed the original estimate.

- Whether any unused retainer will be refunded if the job isn't finished. (This point should be unnecessary; the customer shouldn't be making big advances.)

- The expected results.

This is a fairly balanced method for a job that doesn't involve huge amounts of money.

4. The lawyer's "fee agreement" or "standard contract." (Some lawyers prefer a less intimidating "letter of agreement," which usually contains the same points, and comes to the same thing.)

Some lawyers use fee agreements all the time, other lawyers only pull them out for customers who look like trouble. In either case, these are to protect the lawyer, not you—and there's no such thing as a "standard contract," no matter how official it looks. The lawyer's fee agreement may be acceptable, even fair, if it covers the points in #3 and doesn't add in any unpleasant extra clauses.

You probably shouldn't sign it at the lawyer's office, though; take it home and read it. If the contract isn't clear, consider yourself warned, and choose another lawyer. Alternatively, take it home and start crossing out the things you don't like. Add in the details that seem important to you (like the points mentioned above). However—tell the lawyer that you're going to "make a couple of changes," and see if he agrees to look at the revised version. No sense in wasting an evening.

5. The complete, reasonable contract, designed for the average customer. It may exist; I've never seen it.

6. A careful business contract, in the form of a letter of agreement, to be signed by the lawyer and returned to the customer. An example of this contract-in-a-letter can be found in the appendix.

7. A four-page contract photocopied from the back of an aggressive consumer advice book. If it takes a lawyer an hour to read the contract and fill the little boxes, he has just lost an hour of billable time. Most lawyers won't do it, regardless of their honesty. Aside from the lost time, any sane businessman is wary of "consumer activist" customers.

8. The big, big exception: contingency fee cases. A contingency deal means that—by any normal reckoning—you have gone into business with the lawyer.

Absolutely forget the "gentleman's club" atmosphere when you hire a lawyer on contingency. You want a contract that specifies the lawyer's percentage of the take—and all other costs, including copies, court costs, investigators, mail, messengers, telephone, and transportation; also whether expenses will be deducted from the award before or after the attorney's fee is deducted—<u>and you want to understand the arithmetic.</u>

The times they are a'changing.

Some states now require lawyers to have written contracts with customers—most of the time, anyway, typically for: 1. A new customer, 2. Who is not a corporation, 3. With a job over $1,000, 4. Unless the customer signs a waiver of contract.

These rules may even require them to specify what, when, and how much, give or take a bit.

But not that much.

Some of the rules requiring written contracts are new, some are old, but there seems to be a common ground: I rarely read of a lawyer being penalized for failing to get a contract, under any rule or law.

Even with the newer rules, the lawyer is usually allowed to collect a "reasonable fee" if he fails to get a contract and the customer later fires him. When customer and lawyer slug it out in court, the lawyers *always* tell the judge the fee is reasonable. And judges frequently agree with the lawyers.

Legal reform seems to coming on. But it hasn't happened yet, and when it does, there will be millions of brush-fire skirmishes as the lawyers fight a rearguard campaign.

EXPERIENCE vs. COMPETENCE

An impossible choice. If you can only have one, choose competence. But try like the devil for both.

Also see USING ONE LAWYER TO CONTROL ANOTHER *(p.169)*.

LOCAL KNOWLEDGE AND CONNECTIONS

Either one can be critical.

Local knowledge can prevent big mistakes. Don't learn the hard way that your city slicker lawyer missed something the worst lawyer in Podunk could have told you.

The general rules:

- Get a lawyer who knows the ballpark—whether that's Montana politics, a Municipal Court in Texas, Superior Court in New York, or the back corridors of the U.S. Capitol.

- If you're trying to get something *done*, out in the real world, it's better to have a lawyer who's right inside the ballpark. If you're going to court, the lawyer's raw ability becomes more important.

Local connections can be equally useful: a permit may appear magically, a criminal case may never reach trial, bureaucratic meddling may be stopped at a higher level, or the bank may have money to lend after all.

Careful, though. Networks can be dangerous to an outsider. If you're bucking the establishment, ask yourself: Where are the lawyer's long-term interests? If his interests are in the wrong place, a determined outside lawyer might be best. (See SELLOUTS, p.166.)

It's nice to see that your lawyer is on good terms with the judge; it's less comforting to find that he belongs to the same golf club as the guy suing you. When dealing with good ole boys, I'm always reminded of the man who tried to take over Chemical Bank some years ago, thinking it was a friendless company, and later commented, "I always knew there was an establishment, but I used to think I was part of it."

SERVICE IS DEFINED BEFORE YOU WALK IN THE DOOR

Any business falls into a habit of providing a service aimed at its average customer, and from then on, that's what most of the customers get.

Lawyers with middle-income customers tend to produce a middle-of-the-road service. Whether a customer can afford a more sophisticated service is irrelevant. The ability of the lawyer is usually irrelevant. This doesn't mean they blunder more often than high-dollar hotshots, just that the typical product is less sophisticated.

Lawyers who work for people with money are in the habit of producing a more sophisticated service, plus more customizing.

Lawyers who work for non-profit or government organizations vary. It often depends on the organization's budget.

And a specialist usually has a higher definition of service.

This doesn't have that much to do with quality (how well the service serves the customer), rates, or the final bill. Steak isn't automatically better than hamburger, and hamburger isn't automatically cheaper than steak.

SPECIALIZATION vs. EXPERIENCE vs. KNOW-HOW

Specialization *n.* the pursuit of some special line of work or study.

A good place to start, with no better leads. At least it means the lawyer took a course or passed a test. But it doesn't tell you how much nuts and bolts practice he has. "Pursuit" isn't the same as "capture."

Experience *n.* the process or fact of personally observing, encountering, or undergoing something.

Getting warmer—yet experience is a funny creature. Mixed with other qualities, it opens the last door to excellence; by itself, it's nothing. So welcome it when you find it, consider it a necessity when you need the best—but don't trust it to do the job alone.

Know-how *n.* knowledge of how to do something.

This is it. Toss in a dash of experience, a pinch of tenacity, and you're well on the way to good results.

Of course, it's easier to claim know-how than specialization, even though know-how is the genuine article. There should be some source for the knowledge, whether it's experience, a very unusual school, or a lot of nuts and bolts reading.

My apologies to enthusiasm—but enthusiasm can only be a substitute for know-how if the lawyer meets two other tests:

1. Thoroughness.

2. He won't bill for the time spent learning.

WHAT A LAWYER KNOWS
THAT YOU DON'T

These are listed according to how long they take to learn.

- The jargon needed to read mumbo-jumbo, and read it quickly.

- How to find legal information (do research). But if you know jargon and the basic research methods you can learn to do it as well as a garden-variety lawyer.

- A basic understanding of fundamental legal concepts (the big legal picture).

- A greater quantity of laws, which may or may not be pertinent to your legal situation.

- The structure of law: how laws stack upon each other, link together, reinforce each other, nullify each other. E.g. loopholes.

- Procedure—the way the system works; how to use it and misuse it. This type of know-how is hard to find in books.

Jargon can be picked up reading how-to books on your lunch hour; procedure takes more time than the average person can spare.

Additional knowledge a lawyer may have picked up on the job:

- Which judges are good (for you, that is).

- The reputation of businesses in his area of specialization. A lawyer may not be able to tell you which ones are honest or competent, since he hears more horror stories than success stories, but he should know which ones the customers sue regularly, and perhaps which businesses are moving toward bankruptcy.

- How the game is being played, in his area of specialization.
See BUSINESS KNOWLEDGE (p. 8).

- Local politics.

WHAT ALMOST ANY LAWYER CAN DO— THAT YOU CAN'T

Things a Lawyer Can Probably Do Better Than You

- Argue in court, especially if the judge is hostile to "laymen." And the judge usually is hostile.

- Estimate the odds in court.

- Direct minions in legal research.

- Demonstrate that you're looking for trouble.

- Get information out of other lawyers. You can learn surprising things about your own trade.

Things a Lawyer Can Always Do Better

- Visit you in jail when they won't even let your mother in.

Billing

*"A bill is like a Ouija board. You move the pen until the
right numbers appear."*   Traditional

The idea of hourly records was introduced in the 1950's, as an efficiency tool. Lawyers were not ready for efficiency, and they converted
it to an abusive billing method. Where is it going now? There are two
central forces at work.

Lawyers are experimenting with new billing methods. There are cries
within the legal industry that hourly rate billing is inefficient and un-
fair (yes, *within* the industry). This is nonsense. There's nothing inher-
ently wrong with hourly billing; it's how the seller uses it. *Any* method
can be abused.

Left to themselves, lawyers will abuse the new methods. To a large extent, that's why "alternative billing" is being considered—as a new
way to deceive the public (which is beginning to balk at rising legal
costs). The goal is to mix every possible method of billing together in
one indecipherable mess which will generate maximum profits.

Customers are comparison shopping. It's hard to say what balance will
be reached, though there are many theories. It doesn't really matter
where the individual customer is concerned, because of the one certainty: lawyers are not planning to take a cut in their annual income.
Whomever you hire is going to want more of your money than the
plumber does.

So much for the future. Since it hasn't happened yet, the thing is to
move on to your immediate situation with . . .

A UNIVERSAL THEORY OF BILL CONTROL

Part One

Define the job. Take a look at the legal situation. See what solutions the lawyer is offering. With the alternatives in front of you, it's easier to trim unnecessary work off the job, or handle the job in a different way—or skip it completely.

Would you leave your car at a repair shop with a note that said, "Please fix the car?" Would you go to a car salesman and say, "I need a car but I'm not sure what kind?" (Yes, some people do—but life doesn't treat these people kindly.)

Defining the job tends to lead on towards hiring a specialist. While neither specialization nor experience is as reliable as know-how, either one should reduce the billable hours: the right phone numbers are already in the lawyer's Rolodex, the forms in the file cabinet, and the right books on the shelf. If nothing else, the lawyer is set up to do the job.

See INTERVIEWING *(p. 101) and* DESCRIBING PROBLEMS *(p.64)*.

Part Two

A quote, or estimate, or ballpark estimate. There isn't any other reliable way to calculate costs. Guesswork based on hourly rates leads to unpleasant surprises.

Where the accuracy of quotes is concerned, there are two types of legal work. There are jobs that can go smoothly from A to Z, such as incorporating a business, or doing a tax return, or an uncontested divorce. There are jobs that almost never go smoothly, such as defending that new corporation against a suit, hassling with a mindless IRS auditor over that same tax return, or fighting over child custody in a less amicable divorce. When there is a third party involved, costs rise. Nevertheless, the lawyer should have a better estimate than the customer. Maybe not on the phone, but before he starts the meter.

Regardless of how accurate the quote is supposed to be, there are two more questions:

- "Are there any other costs involved?" The lawyer will probably consider all costs to be additional, from court fees to copies.

- "What is the worst that could happen? How would that affect the costs?"

If you're hiring a lawyer for a flat fee, the flat fee and the final bill should be one and the same thing. It usually isn't—you need to ask the same two questions.

Likewise contingency fees. See A WARNING ON CONTINGENCY CASES (p.100) and CONTRACTS (p.120).

Lawyers have trouble spitting out estimates. Sometimes walking them through the process will produce numbers; other lawyers will be hopeless. Sometimes your job is unusual, and no lawyer could quote it. Nevertheless, the inability to produce a quote is fair warning: they intend to overcharge you, or they are inept, or *they have no experience in this sort of job*.

When I started hiring lawyers, I was often too timid to ask. Very soon I learned to ask "How much will this cost?" Then to be relentless. By now I tend to be a bit on the relaxed side, from the perspective of most lawyers—I say things like "Could you take a look at the papers and gimme an estimate?" or "Howsabout a budget comparison between plan A and B?" I vaguely sense lawyers are uncomfortable with these questions, but time's a-wastin', and I have other business to conduct . . .

In theory, you should never hire a lawyer without a quote. In practice, you may—when you're exhausted from interviewing ambiguous lawyers, or in too much of a hurry (I assume you'll always get their hourly rate, for what little that's worth). If so, you had better not neglect Part Three, because without a quote you're two-thirds of the way to being overcharged.

Part Three

Patterns tell a story. Scraps of information show the big picture—when they're collected and assembled. No business is impenetrable—not when you start putting together times, people, places, results, and bills.

In fact, without inside information, patterns are the *only* way to penetrate *any* billing method.

There is a threshold amount: below that you have useless information, no matter how long you study it. Above that threshold, the patterns emerge. The amount of information needed varies, but one thing is sure—the faster it comes in, the sooner you'll have enough. **Procure regular, itemized billing.** (Monthly is about right for most jobs.)

The central information is **the price, timing, and frequency of each task.*** It's possible to build a picture on that alone. Who (lawyer / assistant / paralegal) and how long is part of the picture, but won't tell the story by itself.

This is not a substitute for a quote. It's damage control, and its success depends not only on collecting the information—but in the lawyer's realizing that your are keeping track.

In fact, you need to watch patterns even with a firm quote; somewhere along the line lawyers have been taught that there is no ethical obligation to honor a quote. (Though the psychologically attuned ones realize a customer may be disturbed by an extra few thousand dollars.)

Stay Rational

There is such a thing as adversity, and adversity increases the bill, in any line of work.

---

*A task is something that: a. is worth describing, and b. can be described in one line. Too small is silly; too big and you have mush, not a breakdown.

BILL FORMATS: LUMP SUM AND BREAKDOWN

There are many useful ways to keep financial records. Some are hard to learn, but worth the effort: they give the business manager a clear view of his business.

However, you're not getting paid to manage the law firm. Past a certain point, you don't care how they run it, as long as it works. You just want a bill that serves your primary purpose—deciding if the quoted price was justified. There are only two truly understandable, forthright billing formats: lump sum or breakdown.

Anything else means:

1. The business is giving you disorganized data, not a bill, in essence making you its unpaid accounting department. (This sometimes makes sense, if the price is right. Large companies and government agencies sometimes bull their way into a law firm's billing department—but only when the potential bills are in the hundreds of thousands of dollars.)

2. The business is trying to deceive you.

Lump sum is fine when you're comparing equal products; things that can't be made shoddier; things that come in a box. It doesn't work so well when you're comparing services, which are almost never equal. With a deceptive industry, it only works for simple jobs, or for customers who have so much experience that they can estimate jobs as well as the seller can.

With lawyers, think **breakdown** any time the money gets serious. (A sheet of engraved paper containing a paragraph with 20 tasks in the left column and $1,832.87 in the right column, is **not** a breakdown.)

What is a breakdown? I suggest you go to your file cabinet (or stack of crumpled bills) and pull out your plumber's bills, auto repair bills, dry-cleaning bills, doctor's bills, etc. Ninety percent of them will be breakdowns, showing the price of each task. Most of them will be subspecies "understandable."

Lawyers have been moving toward understandable breakdowns by providing computer printouts of their time-sheets. They are still reluctant to tell you precisely what was done in each of those time units, but it's an improvement over "Services Rendered . . . $4,233.17."

A few lawyers will tell you they don't have computer records. Maybe, but judging from my own experience, and the various books I get from the American Bar Association:

- 80% of the sole practitioners have timesheets, many of them computerized.

- 90% of small firms have computer records.

- 99% of medium to large firms have computer records.
  (How do you think they keep track of billable hours for the race to partner?)

- 50% of firms that deal with businessmen (even tiny businessmen) will send a computer printout without being asked.

If you're considering doing regular business with the same firm, get them in the habit early. Of course, as more customers ask for printouts, many law firms have taken to producing sanitized versions, revised to agree with official history.

Some lawyers are offended at a request for breakdowns. Some are even offended by the request for a quote. That's old-fashioned. You should feel free to introduce them to the world of business. If they really don't want to oblige, you should also feel free to find another firm. There's no sense in having a hostile employee.

Stay Rational

- Not every lawyer turns on the billing computer for each and every phone call. Don't expect an itemized bill if you already got a heavy discount.

- Paying promptly generally means within 30 days. Perhaps half of the customers achieve this. Prompt payment usually makes you a favored customer. (If the lawyer has cash flow difficulties, it can also make you a cash cow.)

BILLING TRICKS AND QUIRKS

Big Tricks

- Padding the hours. Moving the pen until the right numbers turn up. Since the customers may ask questions, there are smoke-screens:

  —Lumping non-continuous tasks together. If a lawyer sat at his desk for eight hours and worked on your contract, it doesn't make sense to note each fifteen minutes devoted to a different clause. But if there is some logical breakup in the work—different tasks—they should be on separate lines. "Phone call and letter, 1.5 hours" doesn't seem like one task to me, especially when each lawyer has a billing computer terminal on his desk.

  —Breakdowns that show hours for each worker, but not what was done (tasks).

  —Purely fictitious tasks. (What *is* "file management"?)

- Non-refundable retainers.

- Double-billing is a frequently mentioned abuse. It means charging twice for the same unit of time.

  —Version One: The lawyer flies to Chicago for Customer A, charging him by the hour, and while he's on the plane, works on Customer B's brief, charging him for the same hours.

  —Version Two: The lawyer does research for Customer A and charges Customer B the same amount for the same research a week later. This second version isn't even clever; it's simply justified bill-padding.

- Billing a paralegal's work as a junior associate's, a junior associate's as a senior's, and so on up to senior partner. See THE TOTEM POLE (p.116).

- Stealing retainers, or money in trust. See STEALING (p.167).

- Fixed fees. Some days hourly billing is more profitable; other days the flat fee is nicer. Some lawyers quote fixed fees to cut down on the hassles of hourly billing—if they make more money, it's because they're spending more time on real work. Other lawyers see fixed fees as a route to better profits on the same amount of real work. (Then there are sole practitioners who are just starting out—they sometimes set modest fixed fees to get some quick ,rocery money.)

- Combining two or more jobs on the same bill. To some extent this is in the nature of hourly billing. And when the main focus is the hours (rather than finished jobs) it seems logical to start at the beginning of the month and simply list every time unit, in order, to the end of the month.

  Combined bills don't mean a lawyer is crooked—but they're hard to decipher, and that's mightily convenient for those who pad, double-bill, and steal retainers.

- Adding a few thousand dollars for "value added" (p.153), even if there was no mention of this beforehand. (And should the matter end in court, brazenly telling the judge that it's fair play. Judges have agreed with the lawyers occasionally, and no doubt will do so again.)

Small Tricks

- Markups on communication costs: telephone, fax, mail, courier.

- Charging usage fees for commonplace office equipment such as computers (e.g. "word processing"). The customer thus covers costs that other businesses would consider overhead or capital investment. (A service business buys equipment either to sell a new service—or increase its productivity. Usually it's the second situation; then the *increase in productivity* is supposed to pay for the equipment.)

- Charging twenty cents for local phone calls. Talk about cheap . . . Ditto charging for twenty-nine cent stamps.

- Billing fifteen minutes for a three-minute phone call, on the theory that an hour can't be broken into units smaller than fifteen minutes; or ten minutes; or six . . . it depends on the lawyer. Customers worry about this. Lawyers discuss it in serious tones. I call it a red herring. While it can make a difference on big jobs, there are much better ways to lighten a customer's wallet.

Quirks

- Lawyers have a tendency to focus on court costs and the $12.00 for overnight mail. Fine. Don't cut them off. Write it down. Then ask about the serious money: attorney's fees. *Lawyers sometimes avoid discussing their fees out of discomfort, not outright trickery.*

  (Things could be worse; I once had to decipher a letter from a French lawyer, which started with two pages of nothing, rendered in medieval poetry, and then moved on to money with "The question of the fees of justice is a more delicate matter . . .")

- Inconsistent billing. The first time you hire a lawyer, the bill is likely to be a shocker. No slack. Every minute billed out. On the other hand, the bill on the first job may be pleasantly small. Don't ever assume the second job will be the same. I have never been able to predict which way they'll go; indeed, I'm not sure lawyers have any guiding theory. See STARTING THE METER (p.152).

Since both quibbling and inconsistent billing are common among reasonable lawyers as well as crooks, look at the big picture before you complain.

ETHICS AND MONEY

The difficulties lie in the general habits of their trade: the incredible waste and destructiveness of litigation, the earn-as-you-learn concept, and the absurd hourly rates. On an individual level, there isn't much difference between the ethics of lawyers and other businesses.

However, thanks to those general trade habits, a dishonest lawyer is a much greater financial burden than a dishonest plumber, due to the greater opportunities for plunder, the potential size of the plunder—and the danger that a judge would agree with a lawyer's $20,000 bill, where he would toss the plumber's $20,000 bill out of court.

Some Danger Areas for Customers

- People expect to be deceived by used car salesmen. But despite 2,000 years of lawyer jokes, customers assume that the lawyer *they* hire is reputable—he *must* be; his office is nicer than theirs.

- People are often in trouble when they call a lawyer. Their judgment is not at its best.

- A lawyer can write bills into the hundreds of thousands of dollars. Yet the average customer—who isn't used to juggling big money—has great difficulty shifting gears from a "consumer" viewpoint to a "contractor" viewpoint.

EXTRA WORK FOR FREE

Many sole practitioners and some of the smaller firms routinely do extra work for regular customers, or just customers they like. It isn't uncommon to get a bill for ten hours' work when you know they can't possibly have done it in fewer than fifteen or twenty.

The extra work is typically buried in the bill. There's no way to know exactly how much you got, or when you'll get it, but again: the smaller the firm—and the more courteous the customer—the greater the chance of extra work.

I don't know much about *pro bono* work (done for free in the public interest). Plenty of lawyers do pro bono work out of social conscience, or because it involves some subject that interests them. However, the middle class usually doesn't qualify on either count.

HAGGLING vs. NEGOTIATION

Haggling

Retail products generally come in a box, and there isn't much the salesman can do to cut quality. Annoy the salesman, and the contents of the box remain the same.

With retail services, quality is a flexible thing. Especially intellectual services. I've referred to legal work as a "product" in other parts of the book, but that's a *hiring* frame of mind. Once the job starts, I remember it's a service. The haggler can't see the difference.

If the service is a small one, a haggler can usually get away cheaper than the next guy. But if the service runs on, or the haggler comes back, the seller is going to nail him.

The basic haggler thinks rates should be changed for him. He doesn't understand that people set rates with a certain annual income in mind. The income goal might be undeserved, but it's there nevertheless. When the haggler goes for a price cut, the seller isn't thinking about how much he'll make on the job; he's thinking how much he'll lose.

The more sophisticated haggler knows that most businesses have different prices for different customers. Likewise lawyers; they have different billing habits for friends, deserving customers, regular customers, negotiators, and nuisance customers. So the haggler tries for the friend rate and gets the nuisance rate.

So much for the hustle of the camel market. Let us leave for the modern world of business and . . .

Negotiation

A negotiator wants to know:

"What can be done for $____ ?"
(. . . otherwise it's not worth doing, just business, y'know . . .)

Mentions:

". . . interested in _____ , but we're not sure if it's cost effective . . ."

". . . may want to let this one lie, but thought we'd check and see what it would cost . . ."

". . . examine some areas where costs could be reduced . . ."

". . . examine a different product, something that our legal budget could handle . . ."

". . . rather work with someone local, as long as it doesn't end up costing us more . . ."

Knows:

The first rule of negotiation: Never walk in the door to negotiate for something unless you're prepared to walk out without it.

A Haggler	A Negotiator
• enjoys haggling	• may enjoy negotiating, but doesn't flaunt it
• is emotional	• is businesslike
• thinks the estimate or bill is too high	• believes that the estimate or bill needs to be discussed
• wants a break	• needs a bill "that the boss will OK," or "within budget"
• probably not a regular customer	• is a regular customer, or could be
• intends to do business, but wants a better price, or else . . . (or else what?)	• may or may not do business, may or may not return . . . now about that bill . . .
• tries to make the seller feel guilty	• doesn't
• knows he's got the whip hand when he gets a reduction	• doesn't gloat, no matter what he believes
• wants the seller to pardon him, relieve his own guilt	• doesn't feel he cheated the seller, doesn't feel guilt
• will happily accept unlimited free work	• *too* cheap and he begins to wonder about the seller's brains
• whines if he doesn't get the reduction	• lays out the situation more clearly
• has no alternative	• has an alternative

and usually

• has no connection to serious money	• represents serious money
• knows how to complain to the bar association or Better Business Bureau	• knows how to play hardball

OUTRAGEOUS BILLS

You've opened the envelope containing the lawyer's bill. It was supposed to be $2,000. It's $4,000. This doesn't put a good taste in your mouth, or an easy feeling in your gut. Customers generally have one of two impulses: call the lawyer and give him hell, or sit down and despair.

Make no mistake—anyone who has the resources to file a harassment suit can make your life miserable. Let's take a look at this, though . . .

What advantages does the lawyer have?

- He can sue you, and eventually get his day in court. (Small claims court is quicker—but then the maximum award is from a few hundred to five thousand dollars, depending on what state you live in.)

- He can swamp you with papers, without having to pay a lawyer.

That's about it; a lawyer suing a customer is not going to attract sympathy from the local newspaper.

What does the lawyer have working against him? Several things (though none are conclusive):

- His time is probably worth more than yours. How much will he lose suing?

- He's probably not as stubborn as you. He's more likely to consider the bill a business equation than a matter of self-respect.

- If he's far beyond the pale, whichever organization regulates lawyers in your state may tell him to back off.

- Malpractice insurance companies don't like it at all when lawyers sue customers, because the customers tend to counter-sue—which costs the insurance companies money. Sometimes insurance companies cancel the insurance. (However, not all lawyers have malpractice insurance; a few can't afford it, and many more consider it overpriced.)

- Complaints can occasionally damage a reputation, and in rare instances lead to disbarment. For purposes of complaint, lawyers fall into one of four categories:

1. His customers rarely if ever complain. In this case a complaint won't do much to his reputation. It won't breed any gossip; if other lawyers hear about it, they'll figure it's just a crank complaint.

2. Ambulance chasers and similar scoundrels. Sleazy is the best reputation he can have; it helps him collect quick settlements. However, he may have several complaints against him already. Yours could be the one that moves the bar to investigation. If he has ten phony (unlicensed) lawyers out on the road with cellular telephones, trolling the hospitals for personal injury cases, the bar association will be very unhappy.

3. Slightly crooked but pretending otherwise. It's safe to say that quite a few lawyers fall into this category. Though the odds aren't good, it's possible that one complaint too many could start the rumor mill. If word gets around that he can't collect his bills, rumors may spread that he's moving to the shady side, or worse, that he's a loser—a chump. In either case, he has to worry that his fellow attorneys will be saying ". . . the clients are starting to go after him . . . think he's headed for a fall?" This is the extreme case, but any whispers can be negative; lawyers still like to imagine their trade as a private club, and in that atmosphere, squabbling with the customers is just a bit vulgar.

4. He's considered highly reputable, but in fact he's sailing too close to the wind.

How to file a complaint: call the bar association and ask for the complaint form. Like as not, some rookie lawyer will tell you that you don't have a valid complaint. Tell him to send you the papers anyway. Fill them out and send a copy *to the lawyer*, before you file it, and see what happens. Maybe nothing. Maybe the bill will be renegotiated: "Didn't know you were so disturbed about this matter . . . while we feel that our bill is entirely justified, blah, blah . . . make a reduction to show our sensitivity . . ."

- And not least: You have the money. He has to collect. If you've never had to collect a judgment, pick up a self-help book; you'll see it's a hard road.

Tentative Conclusion

The customer is in the strong position—but there's a gap in understanding. A lawyer who sends you an outrageous bill has probably sent outrageous bills before. He needs your help to understand this situation; you must communicate. The first step is to write a letter.

Gather the papers. Do you have a written contract? What does it say? If you don't have a written contract, there is still an oral contract, or at least an implied contract. If the matter ends in court, the judge or jury will look at the evidence, decide what the agreement was, and fill in all the blanks that weren't discussed. So play courtroom, as well as you can. Look at the evidence. Does it add up strongly in your favor? (You may need another lawyer to analyze this.)

When the courtroom odds are as clear as they can be, write the letter. Words on paper will get the lawyer's attention, and he'll quickly analyze the courtroom odds. He also knows that you're building a paper trail with this letter. He will understand that you're smarter than you appeared.

Make the letter businesslike and rational. (Good negotiation is almost always rational on the surface—though the sub-currents can be fairly primitive.) Point out that you expected to pay "X" amount, based on [discussions, contracts, whatever]. Suggest the lawyer did not give you sufficient notice of the fees, and in that light your sum is more appropriate than the billed amount. (Don't be too reasonable, though—never for a moment imply that the bill might be fair.)

You are delivering one of two unspoken messages: "If you sue me you'll lose," or "If you sue me you might win but if you negotiate I'll pay and go away."

RATES

The factors in a law firm's rates are:

- Size. Bigger is usually higher, though medium-sized firms have certainly been known to try for the stratosphere.

- The rent they pay for their office space. Chicago is higher than Peoria. New York City is higher than Chicago. (This doesn't mean lawyers consciously base rates on office rental—but the relationship is consistent.)

- Furniture. I've known some reasonably priced lawyers who had beautiful antiques; they bought them because they like antiques. But when I get the feeling it's just show business, it makes my wallet tingle.

- Political influence. This runs up customer costs anywhere, though federal pull obviously costs more than the town council.

- Specialization raises rates.

- Greed. There's no way to measure this without asking for quotes. And ask you should; greed tilts the equation wildly.

The relationship between rates and quality is limited—as with pizzas and auto repair.

The relationship between rates and total cost is even smaller. I ask what the rate is, but I don't spend much time worrying about it. It's just one factor. I try to concentrate on quotes, honesty, efficiency, and preventing unnecessary work.

REDUCING A LAWYER'S WORKLOAD

Get it established from the beginning. Most lawyers have seen this; sole practitioners will be more flexible than big firms.

Two general ways for you to pick up part of the load:

Assembling and organizing the facts. This begins with giving the lawyer a written statement of the facts. Just the facts. Don't write down suspicions. Better to give those orally.

If the lawyer needs more information—as they usually do—you're closer to the original facts than he is; it's your life. While you may not be a trained investigator or researcher, neither is the lawyer. You're in a better position to track down witnesses, dig up paperwork, or figure out the hieroglyphics in last year's checkbook.

Financial Information: Put it in a loose-leaf binder—neatly organized. Have it so the lawyer can scan the numbers quickly.

Actually doing part of the legal work. A lawyer may not be thrilled by this idea. He doesn't want the customer to sue him for malpractice after the customer himself neglected to file a paper on time.

Also, splitting up jobs is usually inefficient—when one of the workers isn't familiar with the standard procedures of the trade. If you split up the work, at least think in terms of distinct tasks, so the lawyer will know exactly what the customer is supposed to be doing.

Still, there are possibilities. The best candidates are jobs that have fallen into the realm of do-it-yourself, such as: selling a house, estates, divorces, incorporation, and evictions. The courts and surrounding bureaucracy have grown more accustomed to customers bearing documents.

RESEARCH

All businesses bill for research—to some extent. Ideas need development; the world didn't get Teflon for free. Lawyers also bill for weak spots in their education. What's the difference?

It's **research** if a lawyer can design a solution faster than he can find some other lawyer who already has the solution. But if you—without his legal connections—can dig up that solution in less time than it takes him to create it, then you can reasonably suspect the research is unjustified. If it happens two or three times, you can be sure.

It's **remedial education** if 10% or more of the lawyers in that field of work (in the same town) know the answer. There's no reason to pay your lawyer for poring through his law books just to learn what Joe around the corner knew all along. Billable education is one of the reasons to require itemized bills. If it's out of control, take your business elsewhere. Try to find Joe.

Note

Billable education is the tradition that both allows and encourages lawyers to exaggerate their expertise—and take on jobs they're not competent to handle. Contrast the law business with appliance repair: the refrigerator repairman won't work on your TV set, because he doesn't want to waste 100 hours learning about televisions for one repair job. But let him bill the customer for the learning experience—and you now have a repairman who will work on anything.

RETAINERS

"Retainer" once referred to a periodic payment the customer made to ensure that the lawyer was always on call, or simply unavailable to the competition (by creating a potential conflict of interest). After a certain amount of time, effort, or both, the lawyer would call and ask for more money.

This particular type of interest-free loan from customer to lawyer is fading away, and just as well, because the on-call retainer (or any type of routine billing) has a flaw other than lost interest: an idle lawyer may call with useless notions just to use up the retainer. An idle lawyer with a cash flow crunch is even more likely to call.

More commonly "retainer" is a euphemism for payment in advance or a deposit. Lawyers like this for several reasons:

- It avoids the distasteful experience of asking for money later on.

- It guarantees payment, of which there is often doubt—particularly in criminal cases or divorces. And then, one can never tell when an honest customer will get fed up. In either instance, the lawyer wants to put the customer in the position of suing for the money back rather than suing the customer to collect the bill.

- It stimulates lawyers' creative billing abilities (since they often ask for more than their mental estimate).

- It makes a good impression on the customer if a balance is returned.

A deposit, I think, can be reasonable.

Payment in advance is not. Yet the demand is becoming more common. Don't encourage this disease. If you have a choice between two equal prospects, hire the lawyer who doesn't ask for advance payment.

RUNNING THE METER

- Over-building contracts. I can't forget a magazine article about hourly billing, by a European lawyer. Though he thought American lawyers were over-lawyering in general, there was one particular phrase that will always set my warning bells to ringing—his casual reference to ". . . the astonishing length of American contracts . . ."

- Passing documents around the firm for everyone to review—and bill.

- Consultation, conferences, and meetings. In litigation unnecessary meetings are legion—lawyers are perfectly capable of arranging a deposition to extract a single fact when the question could have been handled with a one-page letter.

- Bonding-by-memo. The bureaucratic ritual at its worst.

- Building temporary pyramids to handle a big job. The customer then pays for an associate to confer with the senior lawyer about what a legal assistant should do, and then the senior lawyer confers with the associate on what the assistant did.

  One lawyer should be in charge of the job, and all the coordination.

- Sending two lawyers to do one lawyer's job, e.g. to an uncomplicated court appearance.

SPLURGING

- Junketing. Flying to Boston to file a paper, when his law school roommate works two blocks from the courthouse. Then having lunch with the roommate and billing it to the customer.

- Flying first class.

- First class hotels.

- Overnight mail-and-courier disease. All correspondence goes by the most expensive method.

STARTING THE METER

Initial telephone calls rarely start the meter as long as they're short. Whether you consider the call a question or an interview, it will almost always produce some sort of legal opinion (though the opinion may be mush).

Initial meetings, depending on how you present yourself, may or may not generate a bill. When it's in the form of an interview, there is usually no bill. If the lawyer interprets it as a consultation, there is almost always a bill. A medium-to-large firm is far more likely to bill for the initial meeting than a small firm or sole practitioner.

Handing over papers usually starts the meter.

The production of paperwork starts the meter.

The moment of truth is when a lawyer asks for your address. The bill is on his mind.

After a big bill the meter seems to turn off for a while, as long as it's just the occasional phone call. Sometimes this means the phone calls are on the house. Sometimes it means they're saving the odds and ends for the next big bill. Once I received a bill that included phone charges from three years before—three pages' worth, neatly organized on a computer printout. (One lawyer offered insight on this with the comment that "bits and pieces of wash can always be swept up in a later bill.")

VALUE ADDED (or PREMIUM BILLING)

An increasingly popular vehicle for overcharging.

The way lawyers use the phrase, *value added* means a guaranteed bonus for completing the job in a satisfactory manner. Quite a few try to work this bonus into an employment contract; some add it to their bill without bothering to itemize it.

This has nothing to do with the true meaning of value added, which is taking someone else's product and customizing it for the customer—hence "adding value."

In my view, businesses with integrity don't ask for bonuses. If the employees have a bonus coming, it comes out of the owner's pocket, not the customer's.

Partners in law firms will tell you that bonuses motivate their employees to do better work. And sometimes they do. But they're also intended to milk the customer.

VALUE BILLING

Billing based on value of service to the customer. Within the trade there are dozens of theories and methods for value billing. Though the majority of this book comes out of my experiences with lawyers, this was one subject that demanded study.

I read magazine articles and books by lawyers, which contained several dozen methods of calculating value, including charts based on magician's formulas, formulas that neither accounting nor calculus could unlock. Of the dozens, only three suggested that value billing could or should lead on to competition. Almost all came down to the same idea:

Whatever the traffic will bear.

This is a half-way reasonable theory in a competitive market. Law is marginally competitive at best, and then only when the customer demands estimates.

Three methods recently touted as value billing:

1. A set fee based on the type of job . . . plus an hourly rate.

2. Devoting an extra half hour of interview time to puffing the job ("helping the customer understand his needs") before making a hefty quote.

3. A percentage of the deal. Transaction lawyers, to judge by the articles they write for law magazines, have been driven mad by the potential for collecting percentage commissions on multi-million dollar deals.

As a rule these theories are not variations of contingency fee billing— where the lawyer risks his time and money toward a high (or amazing) payoff. The goal of value billing is high payoff without risks.

Firing and Suing

FIRING A LAWYER

Firing lawyers begins to wander beyond the scope of this book. In theory, it's a failure in management.

In practice, it happens. To get the job done, we sometimes have to change horses in mid-stream. If that's your situation:

• Read this chapter.

• Take a look at BACKUPS (p.53), DOCUMENTS AND EVIDENCE (p.65), NOTES (p.81), and OUTRAGEOUS BILLS (p.143—an incompetent lawyer's farewell address is often an outrageous bill).

If you'd like to go beyond that, for either money or satisfaction, see the appendix for recommended books.

First, if you haven't done so already—don't advance a lawyer too much money. It makes firing him that much harder.

If you haven't advanced any money, and it's very early in the game— before you've committed yourself to a particular course of action—it's really just a matter of letting the lawyer float away from your life. How? Just stop calling; he'll soon be distracted by something else. At this stage, you shouldn't tell him off. That generates a flurry of bills.

If the lawyer is already into the job, and the meter is running, you have to tell him he's no longer working for you. If you're not sure the meter is on, see STARTING THE METER (p.152).

I've read different versions of how firing goes. The first two may be worth considering, the sixth may worry you, but the third, fourth, and fifth are the ones that seem familiar. (Note that the first two versions presume you have a court case—hence the Substitution of Attorney form to be given to the court.)

VERSION ONE: The customer hires a new lawyer. The new lawyer sends the old lawyer a form called "Substitution of Attorney." The old lawyer fills that out and sends it to your new lawyer along with "the file."

TWO: Customer doesn't have a new lawyer yet. Calls the secretary and asks her to have the file ready tomorrow, along with an endorsed Substitution of Attorney filled out "in pro per." (Latin, *in propria personae*, "in proper person." That is, filled out to the customer, as his own lawyer.) Customer goes over the next day, picks them up, and goes looking for a new lawyer.

THREE: Customer starts complaining to lawyer about performance. Lawyer spouts mumbo-jumbo. Then lawyer starts ducking phone calls. Then lawyer's secretary starts getting snotty. Customer tells secretary he no longer needs the lawyer. Lawyer holds customer's files hostage. Customer complains to secretary, finally gets to talk to lawyer, who makes veiled threats of lawsuits if customer doesn't pay up. Customer pays up full amount or close to it, gets file back, and stomps away.

FOUR (with a customer who doesn't get excited anymore): Lawyer isn't getting the job done. Starts ducking phone calls. The timeline is collapsing. Customer writes a pointed letter. No reply. Customer calls secretary and says lawyer is fired, send the file. Lawyer holds the file hostage, customer gets on with the job using his own files. Next communication from the lawyer is an amazingly large bill (I suppose this is some sort of intimidation tactic). Customer files it in the folder marked "Nut Mail" and proceeds with job, possibly by himself, usually with a new lawyer. A couple more bills come from former lawyer. Customer ignores them. Lawyer writes threatening letter. Customer writes back, indicating that he has a phone log and a collection of paper evidence, knows how develop some negative publicity among the lawyer's peers, and maybe will see about shaking the lawyer free of his license and/or malpractice insurance. Eventually the customer pays a modest part of the bill, or nothing, and the lawyer goes away.

FIVE: Lawyer isn't getting the job done. Customer complains. Lawyer doesn't try to hide, admits (in a roundabout way) that the job isn't getting done, offers to send the file back, and quotes a reasonable price for the work done so far. This does happen, but not as often as it should.

SIX: Lawyer sues customer. See OUTRAGEOUS BILLS (p. 143).

Avoid all six of these scenarios, if possible. Don't let it go that far—dump them early in the game. See the CHART (p. 176).

Regardless of whether you're firing a lawyer or giving him an early dump, try to take the business attitude (p. 33) to close out the relationship: I'll be giving up this approach, I realize you're short on time, and I don't want to get into a situation that could adversely affect both of us.

If it's obvious you owe him money, ask, "Please send me a breakdown for your hours up to this point."

If you do fire a lawyer: hope for #5, but be prepared for #4—or you'll get #3 by default.

Note

There are four potential problems to any firing scenario:

1. Are your files being held hostage? And do you have copies?

2. Will there be a damaging interruption in a court case? Are you within, say, two weeks of a court date?

3. Do you have the time and money to educate a new lawyer? How long (and how many dollars) would it take a new lawyer to familiarize himself with the job?

4. Will you be able to find a new lawyer? Was it hard to find a lawyer in the first place? Because it could be harder the second time: a new lawyer may see this as a situation where a good customer is being shafted—or he may assume that you're a nuisance customer.

REGULATION AND DISCIPLINE

Regulation and discipline of lawyers revolves around one thing: a license to practice law. The basic license comes from the state government. Disbarment, the loss of the basic license, is when the state government says a lawyer can't practice any more in that state.

The actual decision to pull a license is usually made on the advice of whatever group regulates lawyers in that particular state; it may be the bar association, or a somewhat more official organization such as a state-run "attorney grievance committee." In either case, these groups are run by lawyers, and they're not much interested in customers. (Consumer agencies have little or no authority over lawyers; like insurance and banking, law is in bed with itself.)

The rules of play are, roughly, the American Bar Association's Model Code of Ethics. To read the Code is to laugh, cry, and fall asleep of boredom. If these rules were actually enforced, there would be legions of disbarred lawyers.

There are very few things that will cause a regulating body to take any action at all. The main ones are:

- Stealing money that the lawyer was *responsible for*, such as money in trust. This—if proved—is considered unacceptable by the legal establishment. There are "Client Security Trust Funds" in some states, to compensate customers whose money was stolen.

- Botching a job by missing a deadline, or some similar blunder that just can't be explained away.

- A continual series of complaints from outraged citizens.

- Conviction on a felony charge.

- Telling the legal establishment to go jump in a lake. I knew one lawyer who was disbarred for refusing to take his turn at representing criminal defendants (who couldn't afford a lawyer).

- Embarrassing the profession, e.g. hiring paralegals and having them pretend to be lawyers (the "unlicensed practice of law").

What the crimes are not:

- Botching a job through general incompetence, "errors in judgment," or "honest mistakes."

- Cheating the customer, even pocketing the retainer and doing nothing, is unlikely to interest a regulating body in most states.

- "Forgetting" money in trust. A lawyer can deposit the money in Tibet, but until it disappears completely, or wanders to his personal checking account, it's not stolen.

With the exception of stealing money in trust, the index of outrage is not how damaging or dishonest the lawyer was, but how flagrant he was.

Calls to regulatory bodies usually end with a lawyer-bureaucrat patiently explaining to the childlike customer why their lawyer has done nothing wrong. Even if you pursue it with the regulatory body, they're not likely to punish the lawyer, and you're even less likely to get much compensation.

I can think of two reasons to press a complaint:

1. The faint possibility of putting one crooked lawyer out of business.

2. Putting one more unresolved complaint on record. If and when the public gets fed up with the legal guild's self-dealing, that will be one more opinion adding weight.

The attitude of the legal establishment isn't a perfect mirror of individual lawyers. Many of the individuals absolutely detest the incompetents within their trade; many also detest crooked billing. But in any line of work, you learn not to criticize your own trade. That makes enemies at work, and invites abuse from the people you were trying to help—all this without thanks from anyone.

SUING A LAWYER

Isn't part of managing a lawyer.

Threatening to sue a lawyer is a management tool, but not a very good one. It takes a long time to get him into court, and then what? Your original job is long over.

The time that threats might make sense is when you're trying to get one last task out of the lawyer (before he leaves your life forever). If you just want the file back, or want one last paper filed with the court, the threat may work.

With the job near completion, the stick (I'll sue!) may start to look like a carrot (I won't sue . . . *and* I'll go away!). Even then, threatening to sue a lawyer may be less effective than threatening to fire him; to sue him is to offer battle, whereas firing him holds the threat of lost face.

Information on suing lawyers is limited. See the appendix for recommended books.

Advanced Topics

DUMPING THE CUSTOMER

Lawyers generally get rid of a customer at the beginning of a job, whether it's the first job or the third—see FAST STARTS (p.66) and LOVE AFFAIRS (p.26). Once the job is under way, a lawyer has three alternatives: "abandon" the customer, "withdraw" from the job—or death by procrastination.

Abandoning

Actually *abandoning* the customer (e.g. ten minutes before a trial) seems to happen to lawyers who take on too many jobs, or who move too close to the shady side.

It doesn't happen very often. While the legal business provides a pleasant freedom from government regulation—where providing results is concerned—lawyers have slightly less flexibility than other trades when it comes to dumping a customer. If a job is headed for court, their professional code forbids them from withdrawing if it would hurt a customer's case. While the code is generally meaningless, the courts have occasionally punished lawyers for this particular breach—usually in situations where a stranded customer disrupts the judge's schedule.

Experienced customers don't get abandoned often. In theory that's because experienced customers know how to play hardball, and the lawyers know it. But more likely it's a question of power dynamics—dumping an experienced customer just doesn't seem right.

Withdrawing

Is usually about money, or the customer's failure to get his own part of the job done. These types of withdrawal should come as no surprise to the customer, since the lawyer has probably mentioned money or procrastination several times.

Sometimes withdrawals are due to conflicts of interest. The lawyer is working for both sides of a dispute, or will be called as a witness, or has a financial interest in the outcome of a job. This *can* be a surprise to the customer. Lawyers rarely chat about their other affairs, so if you think there might be a conflict of interest—ask.

Death by Procrastination

According to professional ethics, a lawyer is supposed to get the job done or get out. In theory, there isn't much ground in between. In practice, the most common way to dump a customer is death by procrastination—simply dragging it out so long the customer says "forget it," settles for anything or nothing, and leaves.

(How could a customer just let it drop, when the goal was so important that they went and hired a lawyer? Well, things look different after a few years. Norteamericanos may be too tense in these matters; Latin Americans, more relaxed, allow their lawsuits to stretch for decades, aging like fine wine, finally passing them on to their children along with the house and livestock.)

IN-HOUSE COUNSEL

Hiring a lawyer full-time to do absolutely routine work for your business is a fairly simple question of cost: salary of lawyer vs. cost of sending the work out.

Hiring a lawyer to do—or oversee—all your legal work is a mixed blessing. In theory your company lawyer will understand the company mission. He'll stay ahead of the game. He'll use foresight to limit losses. He'll diplomatically stop the managers' tendency to shoot from the hip. He'll ruthlessly squash overbilling by outside lawyers.

In practice he may:

- Run up your legal bills by constantly calling outside lawyers for consultation.
  Some people say the consultation habit can be controlled by keeping the inside counsel too busy to make frivolous calls—or just telling him "No!" Others say there is no way to control this habit.

- Assert his independence, "professionalism," and "ethics," at very inconvenient times (essentially exercising a temporary veto).
  This is probably incurable. Have an emergency backup or replacement in mind.

- Play politics, cultivating beneficial relationships with key executives—or even the company directors. In short, treason.

- Demand status equal to the top managers, reporting to the CEO. If the organization is fairly democratic, and the managers are accountable to each other, they won't look kindly on an employee who is accountable to the CEO alone. Also, it can waste the CEO's time.

KICKBACKS

Kickbacks (by whatever name) aren't a daily occurrence, but they happen. The rules of play are pretty much the same as in any other business. Accepting isn't hard—"Sounds fine to me" is plenty. But to refuse, you should refuse. Ignore the offer and a lawyer will see you as either:

1. Too stupid to understand the offer.

2. Too cowardly to accept the offer.

3. Too weak to say that you're annoyed.

So look him in the eye and say, "Not interested." If you're annoyed, let him see it.

Don't expect a lawyer to hand over hard cash. This isn't used car sales. And don't expect it to be his money. He's the funnel. It comes out of someone else's pocket.

Several friends who read the manuscript for this book asked me if I'd ever been offered a kickback. Why, yes, I have. A particularly shabby offer came from a tax lawyer whom I consulted about my mother's income taxes. After determining that she owned a house, the lawyer said that I had come to the right firm. There were many ways to avoid the burden of [estate] taxes, such as making gifts to children. (A bit premature, since I was twenty-six at the time, and I hadn't given my mother's age.)

I said that wasn't for me to suggest. Case closed? Wrong! The lawyer smoothly said, "Of course, that's what professional advice is for."

The chairs were leather, the desk was mahogany, and two gentlemen were discussing affairs—but a kickback had been offered, in return for bringing in the business (and possibly for casting a blind eye on excessive charges). So I found another lawyer. Through ignorance, I had let this one go too far—I should have squashed the suggestion hard. Later I found out that I had gone to the wrong firm in the first place—this one only did tax work for the rich.

SECOND OPINIONS

This is one of the benefits of having a good relationship with a sole practitioner: you have someone to give opinions (albeit hesitant) on the specialists. Not necessarily "the odds"—since it's not your sole practitioner's specialty—but some commentary on the quality of the other lawyer's thinking.

Getting second opinions from a strange lawyer is troublesome. Most will avoid giving an opinion, not wanting to contradict a fellow professional. A few—excited by new business—will try to get the whole job, dishing out hysteria or subtle worries. But if there's a lot at stake, persevere.

Then there's the poor man's second opinion. Call several lawyers with the same question (and facts), styling the call as an interview. Collect several quick and mushy opinions. Then lay those out on the table and see if you can come up with a consensus. The disadvantage of this method is that you may end up more confused than before (of course, you can end up confused even if you talk to only one lawyer). The advantage is that it's not only cheaper than seeking a hard second opinion—it's usually quicker.

SELLOUTS

Can happen for a variety of reasons, such as:

- The lawyer thinks you're playing him for a sucker (see p.21 in LIES BY CUSTOMERS).

- The fee is already set, and the lawyer wants to do the minimum amount of work.

- The lawyer needs cash and encourages the customer to accept a low settlement (in a contingency fee case).

- The lawyer is tired of the customer, or dislikes him.

- Conflict of interest.

Sellouts happen less when the lawyer likes, respects, or fears the customer.

The most insidious form of sellout is bad advice intended to ease problems for someone who is a better potential customer than you (e.g. insurance companies, real estate agents, title companies). These conflicts of interest are subtle, because the beneficiary may not even be on the ballfield. It's hard to suspect someone when you don't even know they exist.

A sellout is easier to spot when your lawyer collaborates with an opposition lawyer. It happens: anything from a cautious dance, where nothing is said, but everything is understood—to a situation where the lawyers are laughing about their own customers. And then one—or both—of the lawyers goes back to his customer and pushes a lousy compromise.

Hard cash sellouts are rare. If you're playing in that league, you probably know it already.

You can accumulate evidence (see NOTES, p.81, FILING, p.67, and LETTERS OF UNDERSTANDING, p.80). But the best companion is the early one—a nose to the wind.

STEALING

From the establishment point of view, there are three distinct types of stealing:

1. Stealing money held in trust. This is bad.

2. Stealing retainers. This is a gray area in most states.

3. Cheating on the bill. This is a non-issue.

Judges generally agree with the establishment, and lawsuits against lawyers rarely produce satisfaction.

From your point of view, it's missing money. When anyone controls a large chunk of your money, you should think.

Situations That Lead to Outright Stealing

The circumstances aren't mysterious:

- Constantly dealing with crooks, whether blue or white collar. The lawyer can pick up bad habits.

- Regularly handling money for customers who just don't keep track. Customers that come to mind would include: poorly managed businesses, usually large corporations; older people too weary to keep track; or criminals who pay their bills from rolls of cash instead of tidy checking accounts.

- Estates are prime targets. Most estates are plundered by *someone*— and the trusty family lawyer tends to be at the head of the pack. If you are inheriting money, and you have anything less than 100% confidence in dad's lawyer (or your husband's lawyer)—*take the will and go find your own lawyer*. To a new lawyer you're a new customer; to the old lawyer it's the last opportunity to write a bill. If the lawyer has been appointed and can't be changed, seriously consider finding another lawyer to bird-dog him.

- Holding money for long periods of time—such as escrow accounts opened during real estate transactions. Customers forget . . .

- Erratic cash flow coupled with a gambling mind-set. Though contingency cases come to mind, this would include any type of work where the lawyer is financially ground down from advancing expenses, and then suddenly encounters large sums flowing through his bank account, on their way to the customer.

- Lots of cash money.

- Divorce, drinking, drugs.

Specific Warning Signs

- Unexpected bills arrive in the mail, yet there have been no expenses, and the job is far from done.

- Your lawyer has the wrong customers—they either wear gold chains, or look like the defendants at Watergate.

- Your lawyer's name turns up in the newspaper, unfavorably. Is he sailing too close to the wind? Perhaps more important, is he running out of friends?

- Angry, just plain angry, all the time, and you can't see any particular reason. Are events closing in on him? (A lawyer's life is his work, so it's likely that his problems are job-related. If not, they may affect the job fairly soon, since lawyers tend to solve their personal difficulties with more work.)

USING ONE LAWYER TO CONTROL ANOTHER

Three ways, all cruelly expensive:

1. Your regular lawyer informally pressures the problem lawyer. The difficulty is getting your regular lawyer to understand that this really needs to be done. Be prepared to employ your regular lawyer for a closely related piece of work—so he has to keep checking up on the problem lawyer.

2. Outright hire a second lawyer to hound the first one. Lawyer No. 1 will usually finish the job out of despair; he knows that lawyer No. 2 isn't going to believe his excuses. You don't believe them either, but he can hope. With another lawyer he knows there's no chance.

This isn't impossible; many lawyers will refuse, figuring it rocks the boat—but others will actually be gleeful at the prospect of hounding a disgraceful incompetent.

3. At the very beginning you hire a competent lawyer. He either acts as general contractor, and hires on a lawyer with experience—or just double-checks the work of the experienced incompetent. A lawyer acting as general contractor offers more control.

This third way assumes you know in advance that you will be hiring an inept lawyer. The only reasons I know that you might intentionally hire an incompetent would be if the knowledge is incredibly obscure, and there are very few lawyers to choose from; or if you're seeking the lawyer's connections more than his knowledge.

APPENDIX

SAMPLE CONTRACT WITH A LAWYER

This is a sample letter of agreement (i.e. a contract) from a business to a law firm excerpted from Putting a Lid on Legal Fees, by Raymond Klein.

This is the only book I know that focuses on cost control from a realistic business perspective. This particular letter is representative of the ones big business started using in the early 1980's—with smaller businesses now following suit. Though the letter would be over-aggressive for a $500 personal job, it's definitely applicable to a $10,000 personal job.

FEE AGREEMENT FOR ONE SPECIFIC BUSINESS MATTER

[Date]

[Name of lawyer
and address]

Dear _____ :

We very much enjoyed meeting with you and we appreciate your taking the time to discuss with us the legal representation by your law firm of our company in [the proposed merger]. The purpose of this letter is to confirm our understanding of that discussion and to set forth the terms of our relationship that are acceptable to us.

We have specifically chosen you to handle our legal affairs because of our confidence in your ability and judgment. You may use your discretion to obtain the assistance of other lawyers in your firm, and we understand you anticipate involving [only your associate, Mr. Underlay, and, to a small extent, your tax expert]. If you are forced to make a staffing change prior to completion of [the merger], we expect that we will not be billed the start-up cost of educating the new personnel.

As soon as convenient, please send me a time and responsibility schedule showing each task necessary to be performed by all persons and entities involved with [the merger] and identifying who will be responsible for each task and the estimated duration and time for completion of each task.

Please send me, on a regular basis, copies of all correspondence and copies of the enclosures with the correspondence that relate to [the merger]. Please also send me copies of all filings with governmental agencies, all memoranda of fact or law prepared for [the merger], and, if time permits, drafts of documents prior to being filed or being sent to the other party or their lawyer.

You have informed us that your present billing rate is $_____ an hour, that associates range from $_____ to $_____ an hour, and that paralegals are $_____. Please discuss with us in advance any anticipated increase in these rates. You have estimated the total legal fees for [the merger] to be $_____.

Invoices for your services rendered and disbursements incurred should be submitted monthly. The invoice will describe the services performed by each lawyer and identify the lawyer, the time spent by each lawyer for those services, each lawyer's hourly rate, and the out-of-pocket costs being charged, in conformity with the enclosed billing format. We will accommodate variations from this billing format if significantly easier for your firm, so long as all the information is provided to us.

We will compensate you for time spent in transit, whether within your city or to another city, but we will not pay for time in another city not performing legal services. Unless approved in advance, we will reimburse you only for coach class travel.

Disbursements should be charged only if required by the nature of our matter. In other words, we will not be billed for overtime or rush messenger service because time priority was given to other clients or other activities of the lawyers. Permissible disbursement expenses and reimbursable charges include filing fees, long distance telephone, messengers, express mail and air courier, telecopier, computer legal research, and photo-copies. We will reimburse you for these and any other expenses at your cost. We view such items as word processing, local telephone, normal postage, and binding of documents to be part of your overhead and not chargeable as disbursements.

Any controversy or claim arising out of or relating to this letter agreement, or the breach thereof, shall be settled by arbitration before three arbitrators (no more than one of whom shall be a lawyer) in accordance with the Commercial Arbitration Rules of the American Arbitration Association, and judgment upon the award rendered by the arbitrators may be entered in any court having jurisdiction thereof.

In the event that any action (in arbitration or in court) is brought for any breach or default in any of the terms of this letter agreement, the prevailing party shall be entitled to recover from the other party all costs and expenses incurred in such action or any appeal therefrom, including, without limitation, all attorneys' fees and arbitration or court costs actually incurred, regardless of any otherwise applicable arbitration or court schedule for the recovery thereof.

We look forward to working with you and we are pleased that you have agreed to represent us. Please sign and return the enclosed copy of this letter indicating your acceptance of the terms of our relationship as set forth in this letter.

Sincerely,
PRUDENT BUSINESS, INC.

By _____
Richard Smart, President

AGREED AND ACCEPTED:
Dated: _____

_____(name of law firm)_____

By _____

SAMPLE OF WHAT A LAWYER'S BILL SHOULD LOOK LIKE

Sample billing format, courtesy Raymond Klein. This is typical of what lawyers are sending to all business customers these days.

Date	Services	Lawyer	Hours
10/24/90	Meeting with Mr. Smart re revising warranties in merger agreement	MNO	.8
10/27/90	Research tax consequences of covenant not to compete and memo to MNO	STU	1.7
10/28/90	Draft employment agreement between Mr. Smart and buying corporation	STU	3.5
10/30/90	Review memo on noncompete covenant; call to buyer's lawyer	MNO	.7

SUMMARY

Lawyer	Classification	Hours	Rate	Total
M. N. Overman	Partner	1.5	$125	$187.50
S. T. Underlay	Associate	5.2	$70	$364.00
				$551.50

Disbursements

10/30/90 Photocopies ($.10/page)	$4.50	
10/30/90 Long Distance	$7.85	
	$12.35	
		$12.35
		$563.85

USEFUL BOOKS

All three of these books are clear and rational.

Directory of Lawyers Who Sue Lawyers, by Kay Ostberg. HALT, 1319 F St. N.W, Suite 300, Washington D.C. 20004, 202/347-9600. $10.00.
> Also contains how-to information, when-to information, an overview of the disciplinary system, and statistics on malpractice and misconduct.

Using a Lawyer . . . And What To Do If Things Go Wrong: A Step-By-Step Guide, by Kay Ostberg. Random House, 400 Hahn Rd., Westminster, MD 21157, 800/726-0600. Also available from HALT. ISBN 0-679-72970-4. $8.95.
> Beyond the basics, the book contains information on suing and making complaints; a list of state regulatory bodies; a flow chart of a lawsuit; and sample employment contracts. [The contracts are a bit demanding; I'm not sure how many lawyers would sign them.]

Putting A Lid On Legal Fees: How To Deal Effectively With Lawyers, by Raymond Klein. Interlink Press, 908 Kenfield Avenue, Los Angeles, CA 90049, 800/445-6429. ISBN 0-9617950-8-5. $15.00.
> Cost reduction for businesses of all sizes; alternatives; preventative law; setting litigation budgets. Also applicable to individuals with a big job.

Nolo Press (in Berkeley, California, 800/992-6656) publishes a variety of self-help legal books. These are (almost) plain English books which deal in nuts and bolts: they tell you how to go down to the courthouse and file the paper so the job is done and finished. Like any self-help book, they can't cover everything, so they offer formulas, which may or may not suit the reader. The ones written for particular states are more specific.

CHART: How Lawyers Should Come Into Your Life, and Then Stay or Go

LEGAL PROBLEM

TELEPHONE INTERVIEWS

- Lack of know-how
- Bad vibes
  REJECTED

SOME POSSIBILITIES

OFFICE INTERVIEW

- No agreement on what needs to be done
- No agreement on what can be achieved
- Unacceptable schedule
- Refuses to make any estimate of costs
- The quote is too high
- Wants too big a deposit
- Reveals bad attitude
  REJECTED

LOOKS GOOD

JOB GIVEN TO LAWYER

- **Lawyer can't get rolling**—See FAST STARTS (THAT FIZZLE?) If you want to help him get moving, then ask—with a sincere but direct attitude—if he really has time to handle this job. If that doesn't get both his attention and a willing attitude, look to your backups; go back to shopping and interviews immediately. If you can find someone better, you may want to take advantage of this warning and drop him, even if you lose a small retainer.

OVER THE FIRST HUMP

JOB IN PROGRESS

- **The schedule collapses from neglect**—Can you get back on schedule by keeping pressure on the lawyer? See PROJECT MANAGEMENT and HOW TO REDUCE PRODUCTIVITY.

- **Dangerous Blunders**—How incompetent is he? How critical is the schedule? Three alternatives here: 1. Lead him by the hand. 2. Hire another lawyer to lead him by the hand. 3. Replace him. Read BACKUPS and USING ONE LAWYER TO CONTROL ANOTHER.

- **Lawyer wants to renegotiate the bill**
  Justified increase: It couldn't have been predicted? Pay if you have it, negotiate if you don't.
  Unjustified increase: Can he be replaced? If not: read HAGGLING vs NEGOTIATION, have a chat with the lawyer, see if you can grind him down. If he can be replaced: say that you can't budget the increase, and see what happens. Then you can either negotiate or replace him. If you choose to negotiate, be aware that he may cut the quality of his work; you'll have to monitor him more carefully from now on.

- **Lawyer develops serious attitude disorders**—Read ADOPT AN ATTITUDE and PROJECT MANAGEMENT, see if you can re-establish a job-oriented relationship. If not, see FIRING.

PROGRESS SATISFACTORY

JOB COMPLETE

- **Unexpectedly high bill**—No warning, no discussion beforehand? Read OUTRAGEOUS BILLS.

- **Results unsatisfactory due to lawyer error, or because excess promises were made at beginning** (Not because of bad luck.)—Read CONTRACTS and OUTRAGEOUS BILLS.

SATISFACTORY PERFORMANCE: PAY THE BILL

This chart works best if you: 1. Read the FINDING AND HIRING section before hiring anyone. 2. Understand the job and where you stand at any given moment. 3. Didn't give the lawyer a big retainer. 4. Kept a backup in mind.

This book originated as a reminder list for myself. One night—after signing a check for $4,000 worth of law—I started writing myself a list of "Rules for Dealing With Lawyers." That was about 10 at night; by 3 in the morning a book was taking shape. A year later I realized I'd forgotten about the reminder list . . .

- Start early, don't get jammed into a bad decision. Do a lot of telephone interviews, keep them short. Cross out pushy lawyers, brash puppies, or lawyers who want a fat advance.

- Work up the competence tree; birds of a feather flock together, the good ones at the top. Never ask an incompetent for a recommendation. But remember even a competent acquaintance or lawyer will still give me bad leads 30% of the time.

- Know-how: Does the lawyer know how to do this job? What's his experience?

- Consultations: don't sweat the rates when it's just an hour's consultation. Aside from the information I get, it's a cheap way to check out a lawyer.

- Small Job: get a ballpark estimate, go by gut feeling, make a clear oral agreement, keep conversation notes.

- Big Job: get a hard quote, schedule, and letter of agreement.

- Buy legal services like I buy furniture or garden tools. Give em' a call: "Hello, I have a _____ . Do you sell a solution that will do the job? How much are they? Do you have them in stock? When can I have it?" If they can't tell me they either have a solution in stock or will soon, don't bother; don't go to a store that wants to sell me a rake when I need a shovel.

- Make a backup list as I shop.

- Clearly define my goal to the serious prospects.

- Drag a hard analysis of the situation out of the lawyer. Probabilities. What if, and easy on the "gray areas," please—I need the odds. If he can't swing it, interview some more lawyers.

- If the odds don't look good, tell him I'll have to ponder this matter. Go home and ponder: Do I need a lawyer at all? Do I want to hire this lawyer?

- Revise my goal if necessary.

- Make a timeline, on paper, and keep the lawyer on it. The timeline is his boss. If he's late getting a significant task done, give him a polite to-the-point phone call. Don't kid myself. If it's late, I've probably been put on the back burner.

- If the job starts to fall behind schedule, or run over cost, call the lawyer and have a sincere discussion about where this is going. Call today.

- If the lawyer can't finish the job successfully, admit I made a bad choice, kiss any deposit goodbye if absolutely necessary, and go find another lawyer.

- Read these rules before and after every job.